FUNDAMENTALIST
ISLAM
AND ISRAEL

FUNDAMENTALIST ISLAM AND ISRAEL

Essays in Interpretation

Raphael Israeli

UNIVERSITY
PRESS OF
AMERICA

THE JERUSALEM CENTER
FOR PUBLIC AFFAIRS

Lanham • New York • London

Library of Congress Cataloging-in-Publication Data

Israeli, Raphael.
Fundamentalist Islam and Israel : essays in interpretation.
    p.   cm. — (The Milken library of Jewish public affairs)
    Includes bibliographical references and index.
  1. Islam—Relations—Judaism.   2. Judaism—Relations—Islam.
  3. Islamic fundamentalism.   4. Islamic fundamentalism—Israel.
  5. Jewish–Arab relations—Religious aspects—Islam.   6. Harakat al
  –Muqāwamah al–Islāmīyah—Platforms.   I. Title.   II. Series.
    BP173.J8I88   1993   297'.1972—dc20   93–2494 CIP

        ISBN 0–8191–9050–0 (cloth : alk. paper)
        ISBN 0–8191–9199–X (paper : alk. paper)

BP
173
J8
I88
1993

To my colleagues and students

Whose wisdom and counsel

Have made this volume possible

THE MILKEN LIBRARY OF JEWISH PUBLIC AFFAIRS

Made possible by a gift from the
Foundations of the Milken Families

ACKNOWLEDGMENTS

This volume is a collection of essays and lectures which had been published or delivered over the years. I wish to thank the Harry S Truman Research Institute for the Advancement of Peace under whose auspices I did most of the research and writing. I am grateful to the Jerusalem Center for Public Affairs for their sponsorship of this volume. The President of the Center, Professor Daniel J. Elazar, its Director General, Zvi R. Marom, and its staff were all instrumental in the production of this book. I am particularly indebted to Dan for his prompt steering of this project and for his thoughtful and generous Preface to the book, and to Mark Ami-El, Publications Coordinator of the Center, who patiently and persistently labored through the manuscript and made many corrections and suggestions.

I remain, however, solely responsible for any errors of fact or interpretation that may have befallen the text.

Raphael Israeli
Jerusalem, Summer 1992

CONTENTS

PREFACE

Dr. Raphael Israeli has acquired a worldwide reputation as a keen student and analyst of Islamic fundamentalism in general, and, more specifically, in connection with Israel and the Israel-Arab conflict. A Fellow of the Jerusalem Center for Public Affairs, we regularly turn to him to keep us up-to-date and to enlighten us on what is happening in the Islamic world. Hence, we are particularly pleased to present this collection of his articles and essays on the subject in book form as part of our continuing effort to understand Israel in the context of its larger environment in southwestern Asia and the eastern Mediterranean.

The essays included here together provide an in-depth account and analysis of Islamic fundamentalism today and how it has an impact on Israel's relations with the Arab and Islamic worlds. From the Arab citizens of Israel to the farther reaches of revivalist Islam, Israel has established a new reality. What Dr. Israeli has to say is important not only for Israelis but for the whole Western world, which now confronts revivalist Islam, not only in the Middle East but in Europe itself, and even in such far-flung fragments of European civilization as the United States and Australia.

For some years in the twentieth century, the last point of conflict in the fourteen-hundred-year war between Islam and Christianity was in Mindanao and the southern Philippines Islands where the Moros, an Islamicized Malay people, were in perpetual struggle with the Catholicized native peoples of the Philippines. Their struggle was more of a curiosity than anything else. Elsewhere, where the Europeans and their offshoots confronted Islamic populations, they confronted local nationalisms rather than a world-wide religious movement. This was even true of the Israel-Arab conflict.

In the past twenty years, however, the Islamic dimension has come to the fore, bringing Jewish and Christian civilizations into conflict once again with a powerful religious movement having the most far-reaching goals. The West has yet to learn how to deal with this movement. Dr. Israeli's book should be a great help in developing a proper understanding and a proper strategy to do so.

Daniel J. Elazar

Introduction

ISLAMIC FUNDAMENTALISM

Since the early 1970s the world has been gripped by the rise of Muslim consciousness around the globe. The Iranian Revolution of 1979, the assassination of President Sadat by Muslim radicals in 1981, the emergence of Hizbullah in Lebanon in the 1980s, the surge of the Hamas movement among the Palestinians in the late 1980s, the rapid growth of the Islamic movement in Israel during the same period, the election to the Jordanian Parliament of many Muslim Brothers and their affiliates in late 1989, and the stunning victory of Madani's Muslim radicals in the Algerian local elections of 1990, have all been seen as illustrations of the mounting tide of Islamic fundamentalism.

There is a temptation to lump all the phenomena of rising Islamic awareness under the fundamentalist heading. But it would be instructive to differentiate between a general going back to piety under the aegis of the traditional Muslim establishment in Islamic countries, and the rebellious Muslim factions the world over, which seek via militant means to drag society back to the old norms of pristine Islam, as if a revival of the faith in its old molds were feasible. Both brands of Islamic renewal suggest a short circuit between the believers and the incomprehensible world around them. Modernity has produced much alienation and frustration, has broken old family and societal ties without substituting for them viable alternatives, and has driven people to search for new entities and group identities where they can find shelter and solace from the hostile world about them with which they can no longer identify, with whose pace they cannot keep up, and whose diversity and complexity disorients them. Particularly affected by this confusion of ideas and shifting environments are young people who find themselves thrust from one Western "ism" to another, unable to absorb totally any one of them. When authoritarian regimes, such as those under which Muslims have lived through most of their history, have occasionally loosened their grip on power and liberalized their regimes, the uncertainties among the youth as to what the future might bring become even more pronounced. It is paradoxically within such reform-oriented regimes that Muslim revivalists make their voice heard.

Modernity, which appears to engulf most of us in the uniformity of the global village, where everyone drinks Coca Cola, wears jeans, reads the same newspapers and dances to the tune of the same music, is precisely what causes people to want to go back to their original, parochial and particularistic culture, and away from the bear-hug of Western civilization. Man is impelled, in this universal world of ours, to detect and make his the traumatic moments or events in history which help explain how in the remote past a pristine and pure society had become specifically his own. Historical depth and continuity are achieved by linking the present to some idealized past or concocted myth. The desire to revert to that past, to revive the old, to cling to the root, to detect the source where it all started, is one of the key elements of religious revivalism.

Religious revivalism, as observed above, need not necessarily be coterminous with radical fundamentalism. The difference between the two lay both in the contents of the message they seek to propagate and in the methods and styles of their activities. Islamic revival can occur within the Muslim establishment, in which case it reflects a mood of cooperation, rather than confrontation, with modernity and the West, under the open eye and control of the ruling regime. In other words, an attempt *is* made to show that Islam is and can be part of the modern world. Under this brand of revivalism the believers are not exclusively engaged in the search for Allah, though that is a major component of this state of mind. More importantly, perhaps, the believers go back to the faith as a culture, a history, a focus of identity. Establishment newspapers, and other media under the control of the regime, reflecting popular needs and moods, have restored, or initiated, a daily page on Islamic affairs, and new religious periodicals and books have been gaining widespread, and growing, readerships. More and more youth go to the mosques, women revert to their traditional dress and eclipsed behavior, and Islamic customs, manners and norms of conduct seem to matter once again. Leaders in countries where such trends are apparent (Egypt, Morocco, Tunisia, Algeria, Jordan, Saudi Arabia, Sudan, Pakistan, and others) respond to this popular demand by instituting new legislation to meet the requirements of Shari'a law, and they co-opt more and more Islamic mores and rhetoric in a populist attempt to gain legitimacy for their rule.

The fundamentalists, by comparison, are more comprehensive and radical in their demands, and more insistent and militant in their means. They want everything and immediately, their passion is impatient. Their appeal can gain currency with the masses because they are free from the subjugation of established Islam to the secular authorities of the land. They can easily demonstrate that the society among which they live is corrupt and degenerate by Muslim standards, and that the state machine is plagued with embezzlement, neglect, bribery, nepotism, and impotence, and therefore, it is unable to cure the malaise of those societies. They attack the existing educational system as defective since it allegedly encourages apostasy rather than belief, and therefore it is considered subversive and unable to bring about the much needed moral and spiritual turnabout. They claim that the ultimate goal of the West (and Israel for that matter) is to undermine and weaken Islam. Therefore this is an Islam which would rather break with modernity than accommodate it.

The fundamentalists, among whose numbers one can count the Muslim Brothers (in Egypt, Syria and Jordan), the Hamas (among the Palestinians in the territories), and the Islamic movement (among Israeli Arabs), offer an alternative totalistic system which, if implemented in letter and spirit, provides all relevant answers to the pressing problems of the day. They also claim that the values that are monopolized by the West, such as liberty, sovereignty and supremacy of law, could be better realized under Islamic rule. For Islam encourages generosity, solidarity and social responsibility, while the West and its adjuncts (like Israel) fosters individualism, corruption, materialism and egotistic pursuits. The appeal of fundamentalists among youth and others is due to both their tight organization, which provides an infrastructure of welfare services where the state machinery has failed, and the impeccable integrity and modesty of their leaders.

According to a typology of fundamentalist groups in general,[1] the following characteristics can be identified in fundamentalist Islam as well:

a) These groups constitute a counter society which has its own internal rules of conduct and boundaries defining them vis-a-vis the rest of society;

b) Their withdrawal from mainstream society entails rejection of Western ideologies and values, including modernity, and they often refuse to conform to their society's norms, conventions and duties.

3

Instead, they aim at establishing a theocratic state based on religious law;

c) They launch unbridled criticism against the established religion and its hierarchy in the most virulent terms. Their leaders do not originate from traditional religious circles and therefore they can label the latter as "satans," "traitors" and "sell-outs" to the ruling order;

d) The fundamentalists entertain an ambiguous attitude towards science and technology; they do not shun modern arms and electronic devices which can advance their cause, but at the same time they reject the West and modernity, of which technology is part, in their entirety;

e) These groups lean heavily on their holy scriptures as the source of all knowledge and wisdom, so much so that the Qur'an is regarded as the ultimate constitution;

f) Fundamentalists reject the religious literature which developed subsequent to the Qur'an, as well as the traditional interpretations handed down through the ages, except for items of religious literature interpreted by other fundamentalists in years past; as a result, they have developed a new theology which ignores the established tradition and often emphasize their own crude interpretations of the sources;

g) Fundamentalist groups tend to an apocalyptic worldview which expects radical changes in the world in the foreseeable future. To prepare the grounds for the "Kingdom of God," they are keen on enforcing religious legislation in accordance with the Qur'an. To that end, they profess the separation of their group from the rest of society as an act of preparation for the apocalyptic days;

h) Women, according to this ideology, must be relegated to their traditional role in the family. The sexes must be separated in education, prayer, and even public transportation. Some Islamic groups of this sort have even rediscovered polygamy as the true Islamic way; and finally,

i) Members of other religions are seen as the source of evil and misfortune. This attitude originates from the fundamentalists' own belief that they hold the exclusive, absolute truth. They are typically intolerant towards "traditional" members of their own faith, and much more so towards those outside the faith. They tend to coerce others to embrace their brand of belief, to "save them from themselves," and until they do so they are held in deep contempt.

The present collection of essays, some of which have been published separately over the years in scholarly journals, addresses itself to many of these problems. The essays in Part I elaborate on the nature of fundamentalist Islam, explaining its ramifications in the political, social and cultural domains in the Middle East. They also show the inexorable link between the rise of Muslim fundamentalism and the Arab-Israeli conflict, inasmuch as a high profile of Islam almost always implies a totalistic and often uncompromising stance toward Israel, the Jews and Zionism, often couched in annihilationist terms.

Part II focuses more specifically on Islamic attitudes towards Jews-Israelis-Zionists, and shows that the anti-Jewish hatred inherent in radical Islam is not limited to Israel/Palestine. The ubiquitousness of Islamic vitriol against the Jews and Israel is documented in the Arab media, as a daily matter, in addition to the many treatises and books on the subject that are widely circulated throughout the Islamic world, such as the *Protocols of the Elders of Zion*, the infamous blood libel, or other outbursts of straight-forward antisemitism.[2]

Part III deals with specific cases of Islamic fundamentalism in Europe and the Far East, and shows that there, too, although Muslims are minorities under non-Islamic rule, they can use Islam as a vehicle of political struggle.

Notes

1. See H. Lazarus-Yafeh, "Contemporary Fundamentalism in Judaism, Christianity, Islam," *Jerusalem Quarterly*, No. 47 (Summer 1988): 27-39.

2. See, for example, R. Israeli, *Peace is in the Eye of the Beholder* (Berlin and New York: Mouton, 1985). See also the monthly *Al-Sirat* (The Path), published by the Islamic movement in Israel, and the Charter of the Hamas, dealt with in Chapters 6 and 7, respectively.

PART I: WHAT IS FUNDAMENTALIST ISLAM?

Chapter 1

THE NEW WAVE OF ISLAM*

Recent developments in Iran, where a rapidly modernizing and seemingly stable nation succumbed so easily to a fundamentalist Islamic upsurge, raise many questions concerning the potential of Islam as a political force in the contemporary world. The new wave of Islam is by no means limited to Iran, or peculiar to the Shi'ite branch of Islam. There have been similar though smaller eruptions in other parts of the Islamic world and, although there is as yet no conclusive evidence of their interconnection, a trend is clearly discernible.

One is indeed puzzled by the unrest which has been sweeping across the Islamic world from Libya to the Philippines. Qaddafi's fundamentalism, which was treated with condescension in the early 1970s, appears to have been the tip of an iceberg which had been submerged in the stream of history since the heyday of Islam. Within one decade the world has witnessed Islamic revolutions in Libya, Iran, and Pakistan, and Muslim unrest in Afghanistan, Turkey, Egypt, and the Philippines (to name only the most important instances). Religious soul-searching dominates the mood of many Islamic countries, and the call for pan-Islam as an international force is once again being evoked. All these developments point to a pattern worth studying.

Islamic self-assertion has been the historic norm rather than the exception, although this self-assertion has been largely in abeyance since the Middle Ages in accordance with the political fortunes of the lands of Islam. The current rising tide of Islam flows from a regained self-confidence which draws its strength, inter alia, from the material wealth with which many of these countries have been blessed. In the coming pages we shall discuss some of these factors and examine the link between the new assertiveness of Islam and the Arab-Israeli conflict.

To speak of a "new Muslim tide" is not necessarily to suggest a more pronounced observance of the Islamic tenets amongst the masses, although in many instances this is indeed the case. We have seen many young Iranian women who studied in the West returning

9

to Ayatollah Khomeini's Islamic Republic and donning the traditional *chador*; we have witnessed thousands of young people in Iran and elsewhere, hitherto alienated from the practice of Islam in daily life, kneeling in prayer amidst demonstrations, visiting mosques, and growing beards as a hallmark of identification with their Muslim brothers. The main thrust of the Muslim revival, however, has centered around Islam as a focus of identity, as a universal faith-culture which encompasses two continents and brings together one billion believers. That this search for identity coincides with a "Third World state of mind" and its corollaries of admiration/hatred of the West and of disillusionment with modernization, only adds impetus to the mounting tide of Islam.

Two concurrent developments can be identified in the rise of Islam: a renascent sense of an international Islamic identity, as an alternative to other blocs and groupings throughout the world; and a domestic Muslim revival which influences national policies. Let us examine this two-pronged phenomenon.

The International Stature of Islam

Well before the Iranian Islamic Republic came to prominence and brought Islam to the fore as a factor in the international system, another equally important turn of events was in the making: the Islamic Conferences. Attempts had been made by President Nasser of Egypt and King Faisal of Saudi Arabia to establish an Islamic Congress and an Islamic League, respectively, but these endeavors had come to naught largely because in the 1950s and 1960s inter-Arab jealousies and controversies conspired against the rise of a pan-Islamic body free from manipulation by one power over the rest.

The Arab-Israeli War of 1967 resulted in much soul-searching within the Arab and Islamic worlds and was perhaps a turning point. Not only had another humiliating defeat been meted out to the Arabs/ Muslims, "the Chosen Nation of Allah," at the hands of the Jews whom the Holy Qur'an had condemned to "humiliation and misery," but Jerusalem, the third holiest place of Islam, had been lost. The dilemma grew more acute for the Muslims as they tried to reconcile the promise of Islam as the only truth and the selection of the faithful as the "children of Allah," with the fact that they had suffered one of

the most thorough routs in their history. Paradoxically, comfort was sought in Islam.
At the outset the return to Islam was pursued as a religious-theological exercise. The purpose of the Fourth Conference of the Academy of Islamic Research, which took place during the autumn of 1968 under the auspices of Al-Azhar University in Cairo, was to discuss the spiritual and theological significance of the Arab-Israeli conflict and, indeed, it reflected the dilemmas and concerns of the Arab and Islamic worlds in the face of the defeat. Moreover, the inexplicable phenomenon of Israel's victory gave rise to vicious onslaughts against Judaism, Zionism, and Israel in a vein reminiscent of the antisemitic propaganda of the Nazis. This outburst, however unjustifiable it may be, is easily understood, of course: if one fails to overwhelm what is seen as evil, one is bound to escalate one's rhetoric in order to discredit, condemn, and discard it in disgust.

This international gathering of Muslim scholars lashed out at Israel in vitriolic terms, calling the Jews "the enemies of Allah" and "enemies of humanity," and even "dogs of humanity;" depicting the rampant vices of the Jews as evinced by their biblical forefathers; denying their right to nationhood and affirming their evil and repugnant qualities; slandering Israel as the culmination of the historical and cultural depravity of the Jews; explaining away Arab defeats as a purgatory ordeal bound to generate future victories; and heralding the ultimate triumph of the "Abode of Islam," by force of historical logic and Allah's design, over the "cowardice of the Jews."[1] A few selections from the conference's deliberations will serve as illustration.

The Grand Imam of Al-Azhar said in his keynote address:

I am in no need to make a diagnosis of the misfortunes and sufferings that had befallen Arabs and Muslims. Every soul had been moved by the shock, and minds are still taken by surprise because of the anomaly of this frustration. The bitterness was further intensified by the fact that the unexpected event occurred before a roguish Zionism whose adherents have been destined to dispersion by the Deity: "And humiliation and wretchedness were stamped upon them, and they were visited with wrath from Allah" (Qur'an, II, 61).

11

This attack was ostensibly directed against Zionism. But since the verse quoted from the Qur'an had preceded the rise of Zionism by some centuries and had explicitly referred to the Jews, there is no doubt about the identification of the two in the sheikh's mind. He could not be clearer on this score: "Thus, we would deserve to be the servants of Allah, to whom he had referred and intended to rouse against the Jews, as stated in His saying: 'So, when the time came...to enter the Temple even as they entered the first time, and to destroy what they got the upper hand over, with utter destruction'" (XVII, 7). The setback of the 1967 defeat was interpreted by Sheikh Al-Azhar in political as well as religious terms, for human failure, not divine fault, was at the source of it:

> The catastrophe of the setback that had befallen the Arab Nation and Islamic peoples was not more out of a political ordeal than a religious trial. It is quite possible for the policies of human beings to get involved in misapprehension or to be at fault in planning and the measures to take in encountering the enemy. But it is inconceivable that Allah would grant to the Unbelievers a way to triumph over the Believers.

And finally, a pledge of victory: "We implore Allah, be exalted His Omnipotence, to accord President Nasser guidance and success, so as to regain Jerusalem, as purified from all sorts of defilement and profanation, in vindication of the rights of Islam and the glory of the Arab nation."[2]

Similar exhortations were voiced by Egyptian Vice-President Shafi'i, although the verses he based his rhetoric upon were different.[3] Other scholars of the Islamic Holy Law called Israel a "poisonous dagger"[4] and diagnosed the "mischievous conduct of the Jews whose wickedness is incurable unless they are subdued by force." The passage continues: "No good is expected from them unless they live under the aegis of Islam as loyal and obedient subjects....The Jews, as represented in their Holy Book, are hostile to all human values in this life, and their evil nature is not to be easily cured through temporary or half measures."[5] And, further: "Jews are avaricious, ruthless, cruel, hypocritical and revengeful. These traits govern their lives. They never change, nor are they inclined to change. They always try to seize any opportunity to take revenge on Islam and Muslims."[6]

Muslim organizations throughout the Islamic world, as well as individual Muslim scholars, evinced concern about the fate of Palestine in the wake of the June 1967 defeat and called upon Muslims the world over to lend a hand in the liberation of the Holy Land. A crusade of this sort was urged by the League of Moroccan Scholars:

> In view of the deteriorating Arab military situation in the Middle East, consequent upon the treacherous Zionist aggression...and sure of the pure faith of Islam, although peaceful and calling for the avoidance of war...would in the event of Muslim religious values being violated, or the countries of Islam being attacked, tolerate no alternative to the battle and the imposition of Jihad [the Holy War] on every Muslim in defense of those sancti-ties....The League therefore urges all Muslims in East and West, in Africa and Asia, Europe, Pakistan, Turkey, Iran, Afghanistan, India, China, the Soviet Union, the Philippines, Guinea, Mali, Niger, Senegal, Ethiopia, Somalia, Eritrea, Madagascar, Albania, Poland, Finland, Yugoslavia, and all Muslims of other countries, whether they be the majority or minority, to stand in the face of brutal imperialists and aggressors, giving their lives and fortunes to the cause of saving Jerusalem and the Aqsa Mosque blessed by Allah, and to liberate Palestine and all the Arab land from the grip of criminal Zionists.[7]

The call to Muslims throughout the world to rally to the cause of Palestine and Jerusalem, in rhetoric if not in practice, added a new impetus to the Islamization of the Arab-Israeli conflict. This boost to the pan-Islamic movement, however, came to full bloom in 1969 with the fire in the Aqsa Mosque. That event proved the immediate incentive to the Islamic world to pass from words to deeds, bearing in mind that it was already predisposed to action. The deep resentment and waves of anti-Israeli sentiment which swept the length and breadth of the Islamic world in those days can hardly be paralleled in any religious outburst anywhere, at any time. The number of slurs, libels, and insults levelled at the Jews were second only to the venom at the Fourth Conference of the Academy of Islamic Research. That the arsonist was an Australian, not an Israeli; that the Israelis had preserved the integrity of the mosque at the expense of many lives during the 1967 war; that the Israeli authorities rushed to extinguish the fire despite the excited Muslim crowds which blocked their way;

that Israel, far from benefiting from the senseless burning of the mosque, stood to lose from the outrage of the Muslim world — all this failed to mitigate Muslim wrath. It seemed as if the Muslim world community, seeking vindication of its hatred of Israel, had finally caught the perpetrator red-handed and was in no mood to let the opportunity pass.

King Faisal of Saudi Arabia, who had not missed any opportunity to proclaim his solemn vow to pray at Al-Aqsa in a "liberated Jerusalem," now saw that the time was ripe, emotionally and politically, to call an international gathering of Muslim leaders who, ostensibly in response to the Israeli profanation of a Muslim shrine, would *eo ipso* prove to the world the cohesion and potency of the Umma, the universal Islamic ecclesia. And so the First Islamic Summit Conference was born and the institution of the Islamic Conferences was founded.

Although this conference in Rabat did not result in any measures against Israel, its importance lay in the decision that henceforth the foreign ministers of the Islamic countries would meet annually to discuss the problems of the Islamic world. Moreover, that first summit conference had a widespread impact in the Islamic world at large. The media, carrying news and pictures of Muslim leaders embracing each other in disregard of their traditional rifts and jealousies, left the impression of a truly universal Muslim brotherhood, a gathering of representatives of the faithful who had come from all the lands of Islam to participate in the greatest international Islamic convention the world had ever seen.

Immediately after the Rabat conference, another event served to draw the world's attention to the Islamic world — the accession to power of Mu'ammar Qaddafi, the young, visionary, fanatic, and imaginative leader of the military coup in Libya. This unpredictable and flamboyant army officer, who was catapulted overnight to international prominence, emphasized the trend towards the predominance of Islam in the making of the domestic and international policies of Islamic nations. Qaddafi's Islamic neo-puritanism at home, coupled with his aggressive religious zeal abroad, made him a redoubtable political figure, especially as his power was backed with large oil resources. Indeed, in those early years Qaddafi criticized, without reserve, the Soviet Union, India, and other friends of the Arabs for the treatment of their Muslim minorities, and even extended aid to Muslim separatists in Cyprus and the Philippines, all in defiance of the norms of international behavior. Moreover, he saw himself as the arbiter of all the Islamic countries, calling upon believers, over the heads of their governments, to return to the strict standards of early Islam. Qaddafi's growing self-confidence, which was encouraged by his success in the Arab and international arenas, certainly contributed to the crystallization of the pan-Islamic ambiance which grew out of the Rabat summit. In addition, the mounting importance of Saudi Arabia as the world's major oil exporter brought into focus the striking fact that the Islamic countries possessed most of the oil reserves in the world, thus controlling a huge share of the world's wealth in this century.

Following the Rabat conference, annual meetings of the Islamic foreign ministers took place in various Islamic countries: two were held in 1970, one in Jeddah and the other in Karachi; in 1972 they met again in Jeddah; and in 1973 in Benghazi. The second summit took place in Lahore, Pakistan, in February 1974, amidst the exhilaration in the Arab and Islamic worlds following the Ramadan victory of October 1973. The oil embargo imposed by the Muslim oil-exporting countries and the trebling of oil prices on the world markets made the Islamic world more aware than ever of its control of the one commodity on which the industrialized world depended. The monies amassed from the sales of this commodity were of enormous economic importance. The world seemed to be capitulating in the face of this power: one country after another either cut off relations with Israel or used rhetoric to placate the Arabs; the reputation of the Palestinians reached new heights, and the future seemed rosy for those who were Arab or Muslim or were aligned with them.

Predictably, this mood permeated the many speeches at the conference, including those of Presidents Sadat and Assad, the heroes of the Muslim victory. The coming together of heads of states representing 800 million Muslims under these circumstances seemed to generate a feeling of religious exaltation, a tremendous sense of euphoria and might. As expressed by President Sadat: "All we are asking is that the support of 800 million Muslim people be heard loudly and clearly before the entire world."[8]

President Assad of Syria, himself an Alawi, seemed more Muslim than the Muslims present: "The Syrian people has devoted itself to defending our holy places, and has been sacrificing the best of its sons in defense of the Arab and Islamic heritage....The leaders of 700 million Muslims have convened in this conference out of their jealousy for Muslim values and their support for the Arab cause....The discussions will focus on the dangers that threaten the Islamic Holy Places."[9] President Assad also spoke fervently about the vitality of the relationships between Islamic countries, about the relation between Islam and Arab nationalism, and about Islam as a heritage of progress designed to combat backwardness, fanaticism, racism, and imperialism. As at the Fourth Conference of the Academy of Islamic Research, however, the thrust of the speech was a virulent attack on Israel and Zionism:

> Zionism is evil as far as all humanity is concerned. Zionism distorts the divine principles...it serves as a tool to destroy societies everywhere, inasmuch as it invites Jews...to immigrate to a country to which they do not relate, and there it mobilizes them for acts of aggression, killing and destruction....Zionism was an ally to Nazism, and Herzl himself had encouraged antisemitism in order to ensure the success of Zionism....Zionism is a movement that runs counter to historical logic, it is not a progressive movement as some thinkers would have it, but a reactionary movement which follows everything humanity is trying to rid itself of.[10]

The Islamic embrace continued to expand, coming to include even Turkey, the one Islamic nation which had shunned the mixing of religion and politics since Ataturk's revolution. Istanbul hosted the Seventh Islamic Conference in 1976, and Turkish leaders spared no words in praise of the "city which had served as the Capital of Islam for half a millennium and whose historic monuments proclaim the matchless glory of Islam."[11] Moreover, having begun with a "modest" membership of 22 in 1969, the Islamic Conference now comprised 40 members, including such "Islamic" countries as Idi Amin's Uganda.

The Islamic resurgence continued and was further reinforced by events such as the Islamic-Christian dialogue in Tripoli in which the Catholic delegation adopted, at the instigation of Qaddafi, an anti-Zionist text.[12] During the 1970s, new Islamic centers sprang up in Washington, D.C. and some European capitals; even in faraway Korea a Muslim mosque was erected in Seoul with contributions from oil-rich Muslim countries;[13] the Islamic exhibition in London in April 1976 met with great success; and Muslims who visited the West in growing numbers exhibited their newly won self-confidence by wearing traditional dress, by indulging in extravagant shopping, and by delighting in Arabic discourse with the sales personnel.

Those years also witnessed the Moro rebellion in the Philippines, and the 1976 Islamic Conference adopted a resolution calling upon the Philippines government to halt its military operations against the Muslim guerrillas, to adopt the necessary measures for the immediate withdrawal of its troops from the southern Philippines, and to honor its commitment to grant autonomy to the Muslims there. This intransigent attitude on the part of the Muslim conference, which demanded no less than that the Manila government evacuate its troops from a part of its own territory, was to be vindicated in 1977 when President Marcos sent his wife and his defense minister to Tripoli to seek Qaddafi's mediation in the Moro conflict! Thus, the authority of the Islamic Conference, as an overseer of Muslim affairs throughout the world, was recognized, and it took a few months for Marcos to realize that he was surrendering part of his sovereign authority to a supranational organization and to water down the terms of projected Muslim autonomy.

The Seventh Conference also manifested more interest than ever before in other international areas. For example, the continued French occupation of Mayotte and of the territory of Afars and Issas was condemned without qualification, despite the generally friendly attitude of the French towards Islamic countries. The conference also expressed its views on the question of the South Asian subcontinent, the East Timor affair, the recovery of antiquities illegally removed from their countries of origin, disarmament, the dialogue between Christianity and Islam, and the United Nations, statements which reflected the rising international involvement and interests of the Islamic countries.

This conference also marked a significant hardening in the Islamic position vis-a-vis Israel. Israel was to withdraw not only from the territories occupied in the 1967 war but also from "the Arab and Palestinian land occupied since 1948 to 1967." The conference affirmed its support for the liberation of the occupied territories, together with the restoration of full national rights to the Palestinians. It also called for the safeguarding of the Islamic, Arabic, and spiritual status of Jerusalem and reaffirmed the close links binding Muslims to that Holy City and the responsibility of the Islamic states to secure its liberation and restore it to Arab rule. In this connection the conference also established a Jerusalem Fund designed to "counter the policy of Judaization of the occupied Arab territory and for sustaining the heroic resistance of the...Arab population in Jerusalem and other occupied territories."[14] Zionism was again attacked as a colonialist, expansionist, racist, imperialist doctrine which posed a direct threat to international peace and security. The parallel was drawn and the cooperation condemned between Israel and the racist regime in South Africa.[15] Despite the wide areas of international affairs tackled by the Islamic Conferences, the Arab-Israeli conflict remained the prime impulse of these conferences and the primary unifying factor in the Muslim world. Indeed, the summits of 1969 and 1974 were occasioned by two contradictory events that shook the Islamic world: the distress and anger following the Six-Day War and the fire at the Aqsa Mosque, on the one hand, and the ecstasy and exaltation brought about by the "Ramadan victory," on the other.

As a result of the Islamic Conferences, and the material wealth of some of its powerful members, a solid Islamic lobby has appeared in the international arena. Prince (later, King) Fahd of Saudi Arabia had suggested that this lobby be consulted by President Carter in the talks about a comprehensive peace settlement in the Middle East in the wake of the Egypt-Israel peace accord.[16] Internationally, it has become fashionable again to speak in terms of "Muslim nationalism,"[17] and Islamic missionary work is being carried out under the zealous leadership of Qaddafi. When the Libyan president stated at Lahore that his country would put all its resources at the service of Arabs and Islam,[18] few people took him seriously. But the evidence of his efforts is clear: the struggle in Uganda and Chad, where Libyan troops defended local Muslims, and the Libyan support extended to the Moro Muslims in the Philippines and to Cypriot Muslims; the conversion to Islam, under Libya's instigation, of the president of Gabon and the emperor of the Central African Empire; the many Europeans, especially Britons, who have converted to Islam.[19] The series of articles[20] and institutions financed by Libya (and Saudi Arabia as well) to promote the spread of Islam have borne fruit. Prince (later, King) Fahd had stated that Muslims must fight atheism,[21] and Libya's Qaddafi was hailed, albeit in his own country, as a new champion of the faith, one of the greatest leaders of this century.[22] Times have indeed changed.

If one compares the texts of the Islamic Conference resolutions with resolutions adopted by the United Nations and by the conferences of the non-aligned nations, one realizes the extent of the Islamic impact on international decisions on such matters as Zionism, Israel, the Middle East, South Africa, the world economic system, the Indian Ocean, and the move to revoke the veto privileges of the Great Powers in the Security Council. The international leverage of the Islamic countries lies not only in their material strength (oil and petro-dollars), or in their numbers (46 countries and one billion people), but also in their participation in a wide variety of international groupings, including the Organization of Petroleum Exporting Countries, the Organization of African Unity, the Association of South-East Asian Nations, the Arab League, the Group of 77, the non-aligned nations and, until recently, the Central Treaty Organization. Often in these gatherings there exists a propensity for the moderates to conform to the tougher demands of the more extreme, in order to preserve the facade of unity. It is no wonder, therefore, that the Islamic voice is heard, and often echoed and feared, in various international fora, not least in the General Assembly of the United Nations. These trends were maintained, even reinforced, in the subsequent annual Islamic Conferences held to date, the most notorious of which was the Taif Summit of 1983 which called for an outright *jihad* (holy war) against Israel.

The Domestic Islamic Upheaval

The new mood of self-confidence among Muslims has turned an erstwhile oppressed and diffident Islam into a success story. This new atmosphere has had a far-reaching impact on the revival of Islam's influence on the domestic policies of many Islamic countries. Indeed, the current trend towards fundamentalism in Islamic countries has been nurtured, at least in part, by the international success of Islam. And success is contagious.

Saudi Arabia, the best-known conservative Islamic country, has not only reaffirmed its "faithful adherence to the Holy Qur'an as the state constitution" and its commitment to carry out the Shari'a to the letter,[23] but has executed native adulterers in defiance of world public opinion and even flogged in public foreigners who contravened local liquor laws. The much-expected reform on the eve and during the Second Gulf War (1991) never materialized, and hopes for a liberal change evaporated as soon as the war was over.

19

In Iran, Khomeini created an Islamic Republic in which Shi'ism prevails and the guidance of government remains the exclusive domain of the ayatollahs. Khomeini was reported to have expressed the desire to see a ruler "who would cut off the hand of his own son if he steals, and would flog and stone his own relative if he fornicates."[24] He also inveighed against allowing women to teach in boys' schools or men to teach in girls' schools. Predictably enough, he also expressed strong anti-Israeli and anti-Jewish sentiments: "From its very inception, Islam has been afflicted by Jews....They launched their hostile activity against it by distorting the good name of Islam, by slandering it and spreading lies against it...an activity that continues today."[25] Reports of summary Islamic trials, where "revolutionary" firing squads carry out verdicts against violators of Islamic law, have filled the world media. Under the stringent new laws, rapists who escape death are punished by 100 lashes with a leather whip. Even after Khomeini's death in 1988, there seems to be no easing of this stringent legislation.

In Pakistan, President Zia-ul-haq enacted major measures establishing the puritanical code of Islam as the law of the land. He was also reported to have set up prayer rooms in factories and censored films and radio and television programs. The government gave wide publicity to plans to introduce interest-free banking and allow the non-Muslim minorities to vote only for candidates of their own religion, thus assuring Muslim control in the 208-seat parliament. The death of Zia and the advent of Benazir Bhutto stymied those plans in the late 1980s, but Bhutto's fall in 1991 may signal a return to Islam again.

In Afghanistan, Muslim conservatives were struggling for over a decade against the Moscow-supported Marxist rulers and providing support for guerrilla bands who have claimed control over a third of the country. These groups are striving to overthrow the communist government superimposed on them and establish an Islamic republic, apparently drawing inspiration and encouragement from developments in Iran and now from neighboring Pakistan.

Malaysia is confronted with local Muslim demands that Islamic standards of conduct be written into law. To press their case Muslim students desecrated Hindu temples in the country during the 1980s. In Indonesia, too, the government has been concerned about the threat to stability presented by extremist Muslims. A similar threat has been rising in Turkey in recent years. In Jordan and then in

Algeria, Muslim fundamentalists have been massively elected to power as soon as the systems in those countries showed signs of liberalization.

The PLO, although a movement and not a state, also has its role in the Islamic revival. Arafat's triumphant visit to Teheran and his public embrace of Khomeini in 1979 augured a pro-Palestinian stand on the part of the new government of the Islamic Republic. Arafat's proclamation, "Today Iran, tomorrow Palestine," could also mean a vow of Islamic brotherhood between Palestine and Iran that carries beyond the expedient interest the two now share. Arafat had been seeking friendly relations with Khomeini since the early 1970s, when the latter was in exile in Iraq and the PLO had supplied arms to the Ayatollah's followers; this could mean not only that Arafat was disgusted with the Shah's rule, but also was eyeing a comrade-ship-in-arms with the Islamic Republic which the PLO knew would come about when the Shah was overthrown. Yet during the prolonged Iraq-Iran War of the 1980s, in which most Arabs aligned themselves with Iraq, the PLO did so as well, believing, as it became evident during the Second Gulf War, that Saddam Hussein may be more reliable and able to provide a remedy to their cause.

Muslim minorities throughout the non-Islamic world are also in a state of turmoil. The Soviet Union, or what remains of it, is concerned that the events in Iran might spill over its border and affect its 50 million Muslim minority, which is now striving for independent national units in the six former "republics" it controls (Azarbaijan, Uzbekistan, Turkemania, Kyrgyzia, Kazakhstan and Tajikistan). In the Philippines, the Moro unrest is far from settled. In Cyprus, the Muslim community, backed by Turkey, is reluctant to come back into the fold of a Christian-dominated unified country. In Israel, where Islamic existence as a minority is, of course, tinged with political overtones, the revival movement is also in evidence. More mosques are being erected than ever before; more and more, hitherto alienated youth find their way back into Islam; and Muslim sheikhs have been pressing for the founding of Islamic colleges in Israel. Similarly, in the Israeli-administered territories, Islam has become a refuge for the frustrated Arabs who refuse to continue to accept what they consider to be Israeli occupation. The Muslim leadership (the Supreme Islamic Council) in the territories has been cultivating the virtue of persistence (*sabr*) in the face of adverse conditions and occasionally inciting a "spiritual *jihad*" as a purgatory process. In January 1979 a leaflet was distributed in Nablus urging the believers to "join the great Islamic Revolution that has been taking place in other lands of Islam." This process has culminated in the creation of the Hamas movement in the territories, which has taken the lead in the Palestinian rebellion against Israel (intifada) which broke out in December 1987.

In Egypt, it was fundamentalists who gunned down Anwar Sadat, inter alia, due to his peace treaty with Israel, but also due to his identification in the eyes of the fundamentalists as the archetype of a "sell-out" to modernism and the West. We do not yet know whether his successor, Hosni Mubarak, will be able to maintain the balance between religion and a pro-Western stance or, like the Shah, will succumb in the effort to reconcile modernization and its accompanying Western values and paraphernalia with the rising tide of Islam, which seeks to drop modernization and the values attached to it. The solution to this dilemma becomes all the more uncertain because of the inexorable link between Islam (revived or otherwise) and the question of Israel-Judaism-Zionism. If the attempt at balance fails, Jews and Zionists can always be blamed. Then the fall back upon Islam as the source of comfort can only exacerbate an already difficult situation; such a scenario has already unfolded in Iran and almost prevailed in Egypt after Sadat's assassination in 1981. If, however, modernization succeeds, and if the peace accords withstand the initial enormously high expectations of the Egyptian masses, then the anti-Jewish sentiment inherent in the Islamic community may begin to recede. So far, there is no evidence of such a change.

Notes

* An earlier version of this chapter was published in *International Journal*, Toronto (Fall 1981): 369-390.

1. This passage and the following citations are taken from the official records of the conference as edited and published by D.F. Green, *Arab Theologians on Jews and Israel* (Geneva, 1974).

2. *Ibid.*, pp. 5-6.

3. *Ibid.*, pp. 10-11.

4. *Ibid.*, p. 12.

5. *Ibid.*, p. 13.

6. *Ibid.*, p. 19.

7. *Ibid.*, pp. 50-51.

8. Arab News Agency (Damascus), 23 February 1974.

9. Radio Damascus, 22 February 1974.

10. *Ibid.*

11. Paragraph 1 of the conference's final statement.

12. The Vatican later termed its delegation's adherence to that resolution "a regrettable error," but it has not explicitly dissociated itself from it: *Le Monde*, 12 February 1976.

13. *Al-Ayyam* (Sudan), 26 January 1976; *Al-Anba'* (Morocco), 25 June 1976.

14. Paragraph 18 of the conference's final statement.

15. *Ibid.*, paragraphs 19 and 21.

16. *Newsweek*, 26 March 1979.

17. See, for instance, Bhutto's speech to the Fifth Summit of Regional Cooperation and Development held at Izmir, April 1976. *Pakistan Times*, 20 April 1976.

18. Middle East News Agency (Cairo), 22 February 1974.

19. *Al-Itha'a wal-Telefision* (Cairo), 22 May 1976, p. 28.

20. See *Al-fajr al-jadid* (Libya), 29 October 1975, 3 January 1976 and 9 February 1976.

21. *Newsweek*, 22 January 1979.

22. *Al-usbu' al-thaqafi* (Libya), 2 July 1976, p. 3.

23. *Newsweek*, 22 January 1979, p. 19.

24. *Ibid.*, 29 January 1979, p. 13.

25. *Ibid.*

Chapter 2

GENES AND ENVIRONMENT: THE APPEAL AND DIFFUSION OF REVIVALIST ISLAM*

The world Islamic community may be compared to a whole organism rather than to a mechanic amalgam of peoples, countries and cultures. For, unlike the machine, where the part precedes the whole and has an autonomous existence, in Islam, like the human body, the whole precedes the part and the latter has no independent existence except in the context and function of the former. Furthermore, the physiological rules which apply to the living organism with regard to its oneness, the indivisibility of its functions and the causality attached to its inner actions and external reactions, seem to obtain in the body of universal Islam as well. Like humans, Islam has a parent and a line of descent, a soul and a patrimony, a geography and a history. It retains the "genetic" qualities of its forebears, but at the same time evinces environmental adaptations or reactions, as the case may be, to various locales or outside challenges.

This chapter will seek to illustrate the tension between environment and the innate traits of Islam and to interpret the current torment in the world of Islam in terms of the reassertion of its inherent, if at times dormant, vitality against the background of an increasingly hostile and uncertain environment where the future is no longer what it used to be.

Islam came into being in the seventh century A.D. in an environment of hostility, both socio-cultural (the Prophet's prosecutors and enemies) and physical (the deserts of Arabia and the inhospitability of Mecca). Therefore, since its inception, Islam developed the concept of the *umma*, the community of all Muslims, in order to transcend that hostile setting. The *umma* was not merely calculated to create an overarching blanket of identity that would cut across tribal loyalties and parochial rivalries, but in fact generated the distinction between Muslims and all the rest. This created an inner environment around the Muslims while at the same time incorporating the basic creeds and the Five Pillars as the "genetic code" that was to maintain and perpetuate the Muslims' membership in the *umma* and to validate it on a daily and repetitive basis. Moreover, as Islam expanded beyond the confines of Arabia, the concepts of *Dar-al-Islam* (the House of Islam) and *Dar-al-Harb* (the House of War) were developed so as to respond to the evolving reality where vast expanses that were perceived as hostile to the Pax Islamica stood open to conquest and subjugation. Thus, *Dar-al-Islam* became the nursery where the Islamic inherited patrimony could be best cultivated and safeguarded, pampered by its sense of superiority over the non-believers who lay in the outer environment, and exhilarated in its missionary zeal to convert humanity to the message of Allah by way of *jihad* (striving or holy war).

Islam has grown and expanded through the ages thanks to the constant dialectical relationship between its inherent fervor and its environmental adaptability and response. On one level the Shari'a (holy law) and the *'ada* (local custom) represent, respectively, the two poles of the continuum in which Islam can be situated at any given time or place in accordance with the prevalence of its innate zeal or environmental constraint. On another level, Islam plied or rose violently against its oppressive environment depending on the fortunes of the Islamic countries themselves and the high-handedness of the challenging foreign powers. On a third level, together with the concept of the "ideal Islamic state," which was holistic in its nature and knew no differentiation between the sacred and the profane, the religious and the temporal, there has prevailed throughout the Islamic world a pragmatic approach which acknowledged that a bad rule was preferable to no rule, or that a cease-fire with the enemies of Islam was preferable to a prospective humiliating defeat for Muslims. Thus, Islam has always seemed to yield, or at least to act flexibly and pragmatically, when the environment was overwhelming. But when the environment was perceived as soft, zealotry took the lead again. In this perspective, the innate characteristics of Islam must be regarded as the vital norm while the concessions to the constraints of inner or outer environments are no more than degenerate aberrations, which fundamentalists in all ages had rebelled against and attempted to reverse by way of regeneration.

Fundamentalist Islam, in its many facets, faces and voices, is the ultimate manifestation of the essence of Islam, while the Islamic establishments in many Islamic countries represent, for the fundamentalists, mere mutations of its innate qualities. Fundamentalist

Islam is the search of purity, of devising ways to shed the innovations which had seeped from outer environments, by way of osmosis, and sullied its substance. But fundamentalist Islam has to reconquer, in a sense, the inner environment of the *umma* while it is preparing to face the outer challenges posed by the world at large, especially the West and its values. It is no coincidence that one of these movements, *Al-Takfir wal-Hijra*, following the ideological lead of Sayyid Qutb, the master-martyr of the Muslim Brothers in Egypt, spoke literally and symbolically of reliving the trauma of the Prophet by "migrating" from the sinful environment of Egypt in which they were immersed in order to "reconquer" it ultimately; and that fundamentalist Muslims have been fielding novel measures to challenge the outer world. We shall notice that while many of these movements (such as Muslim Brothers or Shi'ite fundamentalists) demonstrate an uncompromising stance, willing to die for their cause, they at the same time evince a remarkable degree of pragmatism as they attempt to transmit their message to the world, using modern Western terminology to struggle against modern Western values.

One major question that comes to mind is whether any attempt on the part of Islam to reassert its norms, i.e., to re-Islamize, can be appropriately dubbed as "fundamentalist," or the term should be reserved, as it seems to be in popular belief, for the most radical, revolutionary and uncompromising elements which have lost patience with reform and evolutionary change and have resorted to violence and terror to advance their cause. It is our contention that the borders between the two can be extremely blurred, inasmuch as in many cases the transition from one to the other can boil down to a matter of various means to attain the same ends. In other words, scholars of the Holy Law who do not resort to terror or violence, but embrace all the same the cause of Islamic revival, can be as fervent fundamentalists as militant Muslims who are at the forefront of the march of Islam. When Hassan al-Banna, in the 1930s, advanced his list of *matalib* (demands) regarding the ideal Islamic society as he saw it, or when Khomeini published his "Islamic Republic" in the 1960s, neither was taken as an immediate "threat" to the existing regimes of Egypt and Iran, anymore than other fundamentalists of other times. Their fundamentalistic import was nevertheless inherent in their potential political significance once the environment became ripe for their propagation and implementation. Thus, a looser definition of fundamentalism is more likely to encompass the

27

current phenomenon of Islamic ferment and to reflect the entire gamut of Islamic revival, from the moderate-reformers to the most zealous militant. Since we can assume that the innate nature of Islam indeed demands its takeover of political rule in Islamic countries and entails certain rules of conduct, our discourse ought to focus on the environmental conditions which have facilitated its current eruption, and especially the rapid expansion of the fundamentalist ripple on the Muslim map. For that purpose a categorization of environments would be in order. However, this categorization should be taken only as a heuristic device to understand the phenomenon of Islamic revival, not as a tight compartmentalization of various aspects thereof. For as we shall see, these categories often intertwine, nurture each other, shade into each other and ramify from each other.

Inner/National Environments: What are the socio-political milieus in which Muslim revivalism can be kindled in the nation-states of the Islamic world? What types of ideologies and what breeds of leaders, and under what conditions, are emerging under the mostly authoritarian and tightly controlled regimes of the Islamic world?

Inter-Muslim Environments: When, under what conditions or constraints, does fundamentalist Islam spread from one country to another? In other words, where is the cutting edge of a successful Islamic revolution which renders it a model to be emulated? What are the mechanisms and dynamics of the spill-over of Islamic fervor from one national environment to another?

Outer/International Environments: Are the West and Israel triggers of Islamic fundamentalism? What is the theological, institutional and socio-political response of the Islamic peoples to what they perceive as the combined Western-Israeli menace? What is the nature of the current Islamization of some aspects of international relations in general and the Arab-Israeli conflict in particular? And what measures are adopted by Muslim fundamentalists to enhance their image and gain acceptance in the Western world which they hate but of which they cannot dispose?

Inner Environments

Up until about the 1970s, we could differentiate between two kinds of Islamic regimes. First there were those ruled by traditional monarchs, or other conservative despots, who had a stake in cultivating Islam as a factor of socio-political cohesion, who gave top priority to stability and to economic development, and who found it expedient to lean on the West, in general, and the U.S., in particular, for their development, markets, trade, weapons, technology and political support. This category comprised such respectable countries as Saudi Arabia, Kuwait, Iran, Morocco, Jordan, Sanussi Libya, the Emirates, Pakistan, Indonesia, Malaysia and the like. The most dreaded prospect in these countries was the specter of revolution which might undermine their stability and topple the regime. In other words, Islamic conservatism with pro-Western propensities and revolutionary radicalism were viewed as contradictory. The second category, the so-called revolutionary-socialist-secular-radical-progressive regimes, such as Nasser's Egypt, Baa'thist Syria and Iraq, Algeria, and Yemen, counted on the Soviet Union for support (economic, military and political) and were, by definition, destabilizing elements in the Islamic world inasmuch as they believed in, and acted upon, the diffusion of revolution as the panacea to their countries' socio-economic ills. Islam, though not totally discarded in those countries, was nevertheless cut to size, tame and subjugated to the ruling juntas. These two varieties of Muslim regimes were at odds with each other; the one, under the meek and irresolute co-leadership of Saudi Arabia and Pakistan, found solace in Islamic solidarity, while the other, under the leadership of Nasser, professed pan-Arabism. But as soon as the pan-Arab fad evaporated in the post-Nasserite era, a come-back to Islam was in the making. It seemed that secular revolution, with its corollaries of Arab socialism and secularism, somehow had failed to deliver the social progress and economic growth it had promised. True, agrarian reform adopted by those regimes, massive investments in infrastructure, the nationalization of the economy, and the development of health and education services had all contributed to a more equitable distribution of national wealth. But poverty did not disappear, demographic problems became more pressing, bureaucracy inhibited efficiency, corruption among the ruling elites was rife, and the oppressive nature of the police-state consumed most of the thin air that was left for the intellectuals to breathe. Under the revolution the Islamic establishment was tame and whatever Islamic opposition there was (like the Muslim Brothers in Egypt and Syria) was ruthlessly crushed.

However, something happened in the wake of the 1967 War. The most badly battered Arab countries were revolutionary Egypt and Syria, a fact which not only cast a long shadow on their pan-Arab rhetoric but also lent prominence to the conservatives who emerged unscathed from that almost unparalleled rout in Arab and Islamic history. The conservatives, who were also the recipients of huge sums of petro-dollars, could demonstrate, as it were, that prosperity lay with their mode of life, not with the bankrupt revolutionary regimes who only brought defeat upon disaster to their peoples. An unbridled process of soul-searching and self-flagellation began throughout the defeated Arab/Islamic world, seeking the roots of the defeat. The process was two-pronged: a theological debate which took place in Cairo in the autumn of 1968, under the auspices of Al-Azhar University, and the dramatic resumption of pan-Islamic solidarity after the Aqsa arson in the summer of 1969. On both scores rhetoric ran high, but the end result was a much higher awareness of Islam, not only as a source of solace and comfort in the midst of defeat, but also as an international force to be reckoned with. The ascendency of the conservatives became evident: Morocco, Iran, Saudi Arabia and Pakistan began playing a much more salient role in Islamic politics than the radicals, so much so that such revolutionary regimes as in Egypt, Syria, Iraq and Algeria saw themselves constrained to join the bandwagon and play Islamic politics lest they become the outcasts. This process was further accelerated by the Qaddafi takeover in Libya, (1969), the October 1973 "victory," the oil price increase, and the mounting influence of Muslim countries, which gave the Muslims not only the feeling that Islam had finally reverted to its natural course of victory and conquest, but that it now had the means to attain those trappings of national grandeur. The mood ran high in Islamic countries at the sight of the 40-odd Muslim heads of states who convened in early 1974 in Lahore to celebrate the new preponderance of Islam. But the new mood was one of impatience too. The success story of Islam required that it be implemented in state affairs here and now. Gradual reform, such as that adopted by the *Salafiyya* (the Predecessors) three or four generations ago, had been defensive in import, for it merely sought to ward off the onslaught of European ideas. Now, overturning things in one stroke was the most appealing alternative. Islam and revolution, which used to be antagonistic to each other, became happily wed.

Qaddafi, and then Khomeini, have shown that this marriage was possible. Thus, the categories of regimes in Islamic countries would be reshuffled: on the one hand, those who had incurred an Islamic revolution (Libya and then Iran) and, on the other hand, those who were terrified by such prospects, primarily because that would signify the end of their rule. In other words, one might say that the new Islamic revolutionaries were riding the tide of the new Islamic fervor which has been sweeping the Islamic world, while the others have been attempting to stem it, partly by responding, in varying degrees, to popular demands for re-Islamization (Pakistan, Malaysia, Egypt, Morocco, Sudan, etc.). The paradox is that the more they give in to re-Islamization, the louder the clamoring for more Islam; and the more liberalism in response to the needs of the people, the more pressing the demands of popular Islam. Conversely, only under such utterly oppressive and ruthless regimes as Syria's and Iraq's could Islam be kept in check.

Re-Islamization is, again paradoxically, fueled by the state-controlled media in most of these countries (special pages in newspapers and special broadcasts over the radio and television). The state wants to control the tide by giving in a little, only to end up spreading the Islamic message even more. For this revival is an authentic, spontaneous, grass-roots *vox populi*, not the monopoly of any particular class or social stream. Urban bourgeoisie, intellectuals, workers old and young, all seem to have succumbed to its appeal and promise in varying degrees of intensity and commitment, all except the ruling elites, for whom yielding all the way to Islam would mean the end of their rule, and sometimes of their lives. It seems that the first converts were, for the most part, those who were disgusted with the revolutionary regimes which had promised much and delivered little. Even such a moderate as Sadat was deemed stained by the sins of Egypt's faltering revolution, and he was gunned down to the regret of very few of his countrymen. In his book *The Ten Errors: from Nasser to Sadat*, a prominent Egyptian historian, Dr. Ibrahim Abaza, advanced the claim that the bullet that killed Sadat, at the hands of Muslim fundamentalists, was in fact directed against the tyranny that had been cultivated by the Revolution since its inception. The bullets, he said, expressed the absolute rejection of the entire revolutionary experiment, because it had been a dismal failure.

31

A corollary of radical revolutionary rule was secularism, which had sought to divorce state from religion. Nasser abrogated Shari'a law as the sole source of Egypt's legal system. Though not quite as boldly, the conservative regimes of the Islamic world (pre-revolutionary Iran, Pakistan, Indonesia) also experimented with various degrees of secularism and Western ideas. But since the Islamic establishment in those countries, except for Iran, was mute or too meek to confront the authorities, new popular leaders emerged who vociferously and successfully directed the masses to a more radical Islam that was headed by non-establishment *'ulama*, usually respected teachers and preachers, who soon commanded a respectable following (in Egypt, Iran, Indonesia, Malaysia and other places). It turned out that rejection of secularism and other Western "isms" by those societies which had remained Muslim at heart, beneath the shallow veneer of revolution and socialism, had been a predisposing step for the diffusion of fundamentalism.

Another major factor was the growing social disparity, for the fundamentalists not only rejected the existing regimes as godless and tyrannical, but also espoused an ideal egalitarianism, a sort of Robin-Hoodism which takes away from the privileged and gives to the deprived. Indeed, in many countries where fundamentalism is rife (e.g., Egypt, Iran, Pakistan, Algeria, Sudan) poverty is appalling, demographic problems remain unresolved, and the distribution of wealth uneven. All those disaffected lumpen-proletariat, who left the impoverished villages to seek their fortunes in the big cities, became squatters in squalid neighborhoods, living in lethargy and misery, without future or promise. The promise of Islam, which will assuredly depose the corrupt rulers and usher in an Islamic era of plenty and equity, not only exacerbates the feelings of hatred towards the tyrants who lead their luxurious lives in blatant disregard of the masses' needs, but also rallies the dispossessed and the wretched of the earth to its flag.

The dissemination of the Islamic message within Muslim nation-states is achieved through the extensive use of sermons, Islamic symbolism and vocabulary, the media and specific publications, and organizational lodges which operate clandestinely, all cleverly orchestrated by venerated imams of impeccable personal integrity and renown scholarly reputation, whose life can be a model to emulate. They do not shun problems of the day, and in that regard they are far from the "medieval obscurantist" image that some of their detractors conveniently impute to them. If one scans through various issues of the *Da'wa* (The Call) or the *I'tisam* (Religious Zeal), for example, one finds an amazing array of topics: modernity, Western ideas, technology, foreign policy, social and economic reform, etc., all tackled aggressively and fearlessly, firmly and logically. The fundamentalist teachers know that they have a lesson to teach, a message to transmit, problems to elucidate, and they go about it relentlessly, finding a path to the hearts and minds of their diversified, and growing, constituencies. Their lodges, which are underground in times of adversity, can surface when allowed to operate in the open.

These various means of dissemination usually couple a stern demand for restoration of Shari'a law with a violent refutation of modernization and Western norms in general, and they make use of the traditional (and attractive) worldview of Islam, such as the division between the Abode of Islam and the Territory of War, *jihad*, the Believers and the Unfaithful, etc. This rhetoric sharpens the differences between the Muslims and the rest in the eyes of fundamentalist constituencies, and at the same time brings into focus the malleability of the present rulers towards the West and its mores. The fundamentalists never relent from reminding their audiences that Islam had attained its apogee when *'asabiyya (esprit-de-corps)* was at its height, the spirit of Islam unbreakable, and therefore its polity was invincible. Thus, fundamentalists do not merely demand reforms of an Islamic nature within the existing system, but rather a total overhauling of their societies, the scrapping of the existing base and the adoption of the "Islamic alternative."

The appeal of the fundamentalists can gain wide currency because of the evidence that the societies among which they live are corrupt and degenerate and that the state machineries are plagued with embezzlement, neglect, bribery and nepotism, and therefore are unable to cure the malaise of society. They also attack the existing educational system as defective since it encourages apostasy rather than belief, and therefore is subversive and cannot be counted on to bring about a spiritual and moral turnabout. They claim that the ultimate goal of the West is to weaken and eliminate Islam; they view the educational system, with the help of the media, as advancing in great strides toward that abysmal goal. By contrast, their Islam, being a holistic system, offers an alternative which, if implemented in letter and spirit, provides all relevant answers to the pressing problems of the day. They also contend that the very values that the

West claims monopoly over, such as liberty, sovereignty and the supremacy of law, could best be realized under Islam. For Islam encourages generosity, solidarity and social responsibility, while the West fosters individualism and egotistic pursuits. This kind of argument not only appeals to the emotions of traditionalists, by the sheer fact that it is spelled out by respected masters of the Shari'a, but also addresses itself to the logic of the rationalists and the modernists who come to regard the new message as more promising and less alien than the dismal current state of affairs. The temptation to try the new way, which in fact is the old familiar way, becomes irresistible.

The sweeping diffusion of Islamic fundamentalism in various countries can be accounted for by the convergence between the politically disaffected, the socio-economically disadvantaged and the spiritually frustrated, with a populist state of mind which purports to find remedies not in the established order but outside of it. As a political opposition, the fundamentalists despise the establishment and fight against it; as populists, they strive to draw the populace into their self-created environments, so as to subtract it from the rule of the elites in government. Thus, two forces are in permanent competition for the soul of the people: established Islam, which enjoys the backing and the financial wherewithal of the state, and popular Islam, which is more structurally amorphous (that is precisely its strength), but lurks on the horizon as a viable alternative. So, while established Islam disburses the funds to build new mosques, cultural centers, schools and *madrasas* (centers of learning), encourages the study of Arabic and of Islam, and publishes Islamic books and tracts for widespread distribution, popular Islam lends the impetus to the spontaneity of the masses: large mosque attendance, pilgrimage to Mecca, donning the traditional garb, the observation of tradition, and engaging in political activity. Established Islam rests on the official dogma and scholarship, seems remote, detached and irrelevant to many, while popular Islam, as reflected in the various brotherhoods and *jama'at* (Islamic societies), would rather stress the mystical aspects of the faith and the authority of the spiritual leader of the fundamentalist group, whose closeness, immediacy, availability and concern for day-to-day problems can only draw large followings. An Islamic revolution succeeds when the fundamentalists take over the instruments of government. But even then, their populist strain is not lost: Iran still has as much recourse to Revolutionary Guards as it has to its established army, and revolutionary Libya has dubbed itself *"jamahiriyya,"* that is, the rule by the masses, for the masses (shall we call it "massocracy"?). The new leaders of these revolutions shun all the trappings of their failing predecessors: they are certainly authoritarian (that is in the nature of any revolution), but they are open, accessible to the people, modest in their demeanor and life style, sometimes even ascetic. And their message to the masses is not materialistic, soft, cajoling, rational, this-worldly and modern, but rather spiritual, exacting, demanding, promising little, shifting the emphasis to the hereafter. The fascinating paradox is that they seem to appeal much more with their harsh message than their predecessors with their flurry of promises. In the eyes of the masses, it is apparently preferable to share in a crude and modest egalitarianism than watch wealth unevenly concentrated in the hands of a few. But until they succeed in their revolution, the fundamentalists create their inner environ-ments in preparation for that eventuality. Such an environment need not necessarily be a geographical state-within-a-state, although the Muslim Brothers of Egypt and Syria have at various times built their strongholds as launching pads for the anticipated revolution. Often, the inner environment consists of a spiritual separation between the committed Muslims and the rest of the public, between the true believers and the "apostates," between the ruled and their rulers, or between the people and the establishment. *Jama'at al-Takfir wal-Hijra* (The Society [accusing others] of Apostasy and [postulating] Migration [from that milieu]) in Egypt drew that symbolism to its limit by denouncing Egyptian society in general as apostate (*kuffar*), which justifies their own spiritual migration from their country in order to create a new and pure environment where Islam would thrive pending the general dissemination of their beliefs.

While Muslim Brothers in Egypt and Syria may be playing by the rules, in order to avoid the sort of persecution and physical elimina-tion that had afflicted their peers under Nasser and Assad, in the process allying themselves with existing political parties or forcing Islamization on their political rivals, more fanatic groups such as the Shi'ites of Lebanon and the *jama'at* of Egypt are not remiss in proclaiming their ultimate goals and are prepared to use violence to attain them. In Lebanon, some Shi'ites are threatening to establish a Muslim republic in their war-torn and community-riddled country, resorting to violence if necessary; in Egypt, had the *jama'at* succeeded in assassinating the entire leadership of the land on that October 6, 1981, they were prepared to take over the radio station of Assyut and proclaim an Islamic Republic. In Indonesia and Malaysia, small groups of extremists try to impose their fundamentalism through terror, but they seem to pose no danger to the existing regimes so far. The Hamas in the Israeli-administered territories does not hide its ambition to turn all Palestine (including Israel) into an Islamic state and even the Muslim fundamentalists in Israel, as we shall see below, have great difficulty hiding their ultimate goal of Islamizing their environment. The recent success of the fundamentalists in democratic elections in Jordan and Algeria can only lend impetus to this process.

Inter-Islamic Environments

The established Islam of the regimes and the popular Islam of the masses can also be perceived on the inter-Muslim level. On the one hand, there is the institutional pan-Islam of the Islamic Conferences, Islamic politics and diplomacy, Islamic banks and cultural centers, even an "Islamic bomb." Admittedly, this is not a fundamentalist Islam per se, as far as its ideology, if it has any, is concerned. However, it has had an immense psychological impact on the Muslim community as a whole inasmuch as it has vastly contributed to its regaining its self-confidence and to taking cognizance of its worldwide influence and power. The sight of Muslim heads of states representing more than 45 countries spanning the continents of Asia and Africa is an exhilarating one to many a Muslim soul. The media in the Muslim countries, which carry live the annual gatherings of the Islamic Conference, achieve immediate and direct transmission, the world over, of the facade of cohesion and unity that those conferences convey. If we can revert to our biological metaphor, one senses that the diverse organs of the body of Islam are sewn together, to form, again, a breathing and living creature of awesome dimensions. It is as though a collective Caliphate came to life in place of the defunct overarching authority of the Caliph of the Muslim world.

On the other hand, there is reason for both a stifling apprehension, or a hopeful expectation, depending on who you were: if you were a pro-Western conservative or a "socialist"-secularist, you would be scared stiff that the wave of Islamic revolution might sweep you away; you would be horrified by the vast coverage and attention that Khomeini and Iran enjoyed around the world; you would be terrorized by the creeping Islamization of your society (changes in the mores of dress in Egypt, Pakistan, Morocco, Algeria and even Malaysia, separation between sexes in some universities, the Islamic literature that is profusely distributed in the streets of Islamic cities, etc.), and by the re-Islamizing rhetoric of your leaders who are afraid to lag behind popular demand for more Islam. But if you are a Muslim Brother, a frustrated intellectual, poor and dispossessed, or feel politically or spiritually oppressed, you would be enchanted with Khomeini's success, and you would hope that some of that enchantment might rub off on your own society. You would be elated to see pictures of Khomeini distributed in the streets (in Lebanon, the Israeli-administered territories, and even among Afghani Mujahidin); you might even enroll in the service of Allah by joining a *jihad* group or a Muslim Guard. Evidently, success breeds success. The Iranian regime has made no secret of its intent, indeed determination, to universalize its revolution to the entire Islamic world and some steps in that direction can already be credited to that zeal. Indeed, the Islamic world has been stirring since the Khomeini victory, and the environmental spill-over of that revolution-for-export is felt in many corners thereof. A few examples will illustrate the point: Sadat's assassination and the near-toppling of the Egyptian government as a result; the take-over of the Holy Mosque in Mecca and the ensuing burning of the American Embassy in Islamabad; the Muslim Brothers' uprising in Hama, Syria; bombings in the Gulf States; the rise of the Shi'ites in Lebanon; Muslim fundamentalism among the Arab minority in Israel and in the Israeli-administered territories; the rise of fundamentalists in Algerian and Jordanian politics. The war between Iran and Iraq was itself triggered by the Khomeini successes and the fear of Saddam Hussein that his own Shi'ites in southern Iraq, where Khomeini had been exiled for 15 years (1963-78), might get caught up in the fervor of the Iranian Islamic revolution. It must be stressed, however, that some odd alliances have also emerged out of Iran's successes: Qaddafi, the consummate Sunni, has elected the cause of Islamic revolution over Sunnite-Shi'ite theological bickerings; Assad of Syria, who evidently cares for neither, finds in Iran a comforting ally against his enemies of the Iraqi Baa'th; and Yasser Arafat, at least during the initial stages of the Iranian Revolution, was visibly elated to embrace Khomeini in Teheran and to state "Today Teheran, tomorrow Tel-Aviv!," in view of the Ayatollah's unabated anti-Jewish and anti-Israeli convictions. Thus, the diffusion of fundamentalist Islam by model, or emulation of what seems successful next door, and the adulation of the heroes of that success (Qaddafi, then Khomeini, and now Sheikh Fadlallah of Shi'ite Lebanon, and to an extent Sheikh Madani of Algeria), has often defied the Sunnite-Shi'ite cleavages. What seems to matter in the Islamic Revolution construct is that it is consummately Islamic and therefore desirable, and that it is a revolution, where all means, not least of all violent shortcuts, are justified to attain the sacred goal.

The International Environment

The two-pronged surge of Islamic fundamentalism, on the institutional/established as well as on the popular/spontaneous levels, seems to hold true in the international arena as well, namely, in the diffusion of Islamic fundamentalism and its political and psychological impact beyond the world of Islam. But unlike the national and inter-Islamic levels of diffusion, where the triggers are mainly internal, that is, in reaction against existing regimes or the desire to go back to the roots, or disappointment with modernity, or the result of inter-Islamic struggle for influence and supremacy, in the world arena there seem to be two ready-made scarecrows and scapegoats at the same time: the West and, more emphatically, Israel. Indeed, there are few more effective themes around which the resurgent world of Islam can rally than those two. In a way, the intensity of fundamentalist Islam can be gauged through its anti-Western, and especially anti-Israeli, pronouncements and deeds. That is to say, the higher the profile of Islam (e.g., Iran, Libya, the Muslim Brothers and others), the more acrimonious and bitter are the charges levelled against the West and Israel, who are "credited" with about every ill that has afflicted Muslim society anywhere. Not that there is anything specifically fundamentalistic about attacking the West or Israel, others do too for their own reasons, but by stating something against them, with proper citations from the Holy Qur'an, or from Islamic tradition, or from past or present heroes of Islam, one somehow sounds more Islamic; and by listening to those preachings of politicians or religious authorities, frustrated Muslim audiences somehow become more feverish about their Islam.

Thus, exactly as the Ayatollah Khomeini is a hero of Islam, inter alia, because of his defiance of the West and the unbridled hatred of Jews and Israel that he articulated, so Sadat, who made a deal with Israel, through American mediation, is considered by fundamentalists as a traitor to the cause of Islam. Anti-Western and anti-Israeli rhetoric and action are both an expression and a tool of fundamentalist Islam and its diffusion. One would have noticed that an anti-American or anti-Israeli bombing, public speech, hijacking, or other acts of hostility mounted by fundamentalist groups, would generate further demonstrations and other manifestations of anger and violence by supporters of those groups. The victims of such violent acts (we call them terror, they view them as justified self-defense or vengeance in the path of Allah), are viewed faulty, and therefore more eruptions of violence and hostility are directed at them and their governments. In these instances there is a convergence between popular and institutional Islam: any action taken by Muslim governments and any pronouncement uttered by an established religious leader, if it is anti-Western or anti-Israeli in import, would rouse popular support; conversely, popular eruptions against the West and Israel are often either condoned by the established authorities or treated with leniency for fear of antagonizing the populace.

We have already discussed the Islamic Conferences' interest in and defense of Muslim minorities living under non-Islamic rule. Again, there is perhaps nothing fundamentalistic about the resolutions adopted by the Conferences and other Islamic bodies in this regard, but when one remembers that this new interest in Muslim minorities is concurrent with the new posture of fundamentalist Islam, and that the rhetoric used is that of the obligation of the *umma* to bear worldwide responsibility for its members, one comprehends that the new ambiance of universal Islam is part and parcel of this revivalist process. The fact that non-Muslim nations such as Cyprus, the Philippines and Ethiopia are prepared, indeed compelled, to deal with the Islamic Conferences with regard to their own Muslim minorities, demonstrated to all the faithful the international power that Islam had come to wield. Another case in point is Afghanistan, which was certainly not a fundamentalist country, but its very invasion by the Soviets became a Muslim *cause celebre*. The Soviets may have invaded for fear that Islamic fundamentalism might spill over to their own Islamic republics, but they were to find out that their action aroused anti-Soviet emotions in much of the Islamic world. For the more the Afghans were oppressed and obliterated by the Soviets, the more they and other Muslims turned the war into a fundamentalist cause, with the vocabulary of *jihad*, Mujahidin, etc.

Despite the wide range of international affairs tackled by the Islamic Conferences, the Arab-Israeli conflict understandably remains the main preoccupation of these conferences and the primary unifying factor in the international dimension of Islamic politics. Indeed, the first two peaks in the short history of these conferences, namely the summits of 1969 and 1974, were occasioned by two contradictory events that shook the Islamic world: the distress and anger upon the burning of the Aqsa Mosque, following the 1967 defeat, and the ecstasy and exaltation of the "Ramadan Victory." Israel is in fact a primary target both in her own right, due to the grievances that the Islamic world has been entertaining in her regard since her inception, and also because she is considered as an arm of the West, with whom the Muslim world has a separate account to settle. The West has been a major target of Islamic recriminations, to be sure, but due to its strength, political and military might, and the dependence of most Islamic countries on its markets and technology, there is very little that established Islam is able or willing to do to hurt it. The wrath is then directed in what psychologists call "displaced aggression" against little Israel, which is a much more vulnerable target to attack, to boycott, to condemn, to threaten, etc. But by doing so, by attacking certain attributes of Israel's modernity and Western character, it is clear that aim is taken at the West in general. In the eyes of popular Islam, the distinction between Israel and the U.S. is non-existent. The crowds who took the American hostages in Teheran (1979), like those who marched in the cities of Libya after the Gulf of Sidra incident (1986), or those who demonstrated following the Sabra and Shatilla massacres (1982), or the violent eruptions in the Beirut Airport during the TWA hostage ordeal (1985), all shouted slogans against both the U.S. and Israel, all waved their angry fists in the face of both, and burned both countries' flags. Those crowd are merely responding to the process of Islamization of Arab foreign policy in general and the Arab-Israeli conflict in particular, in which the use of Islamic symbols and Islamic rhetoric has become a fact of life. All that one has to do is to listen to the Friday *khutba* (sermon) that is broadcast live from

Arab/Muslim capitals to realize how lively, appealing and real is the current treatment (or rather ill-treatment) of Jews, Israel, Zionism and the West throughout the Islamic world. No wonder, then, that a country like Iran, which had been on the best of terms with Israel under the Shah, turned overnight more vitriolic against Israel than most Arab countries, upon the ascendence of the Islamic Republic. They even sent volunteers to the Lebanese Bek'a Valley to fight against Israel (beginning in the summer of 1979), for Islamic reasons and to attain Islamic goals, such as the liberation of the Holy Land and especially Jerusalem.

The Islamic counter-attack against Israel and the West (bombings, threats, hijackings, demonstrations, boycotts and high rhetoric) also has a subtle side to it. The very defense measures adopted by Westerners and Israelis around the world in themselves afford the fundamentalists a great deal of emotional satisfaction. The mere sight of the all-powerful, aggressive, colonial, oppressive and exploitative "imperialists" coming to their knees for oil supplies or to get their hostages back, or compelled to fortify themselves behind their concrete roadblocks and electronic devices, attests, in the minds of many fundamentalists, to Western fears and weaknesses, which in turn encourage further attacks and more daring in carrying them out. Paradoxically, however, being aware of Western might, attempts are being made by some Islamic circles to cajole it, cater to it and pacify it by appealing to its values and sensitivities: human rights, freedom, reasoning, equality, fairness and the like. Indeed, side by side with the manifestations of hostility and violence towards the West, one is struck by the large variety of Islamic peaceful activity in and towards the West: the Islamic-Christian dialogue, new centers of Islamic worship and culture in the U.S. and major European cities, Islamic conferences and exhibitions around the Western world, multi-page ads in major Western newspapers and magazines, and an attempt to explain the world of Islam, subtly furthering the fundamentalist cause by using Western value-loaded vocabulary (incidentally, none of this is done in either the Third World or the Soviet Bloc). For example: in the name of freedom of worship, a Saudi-funded mosque and cultural center can be erected in some Western city, while the same freedom cannot be afforded to Christians (let alone Jews) to build houses of worship in Saudi territory; Lebanese hijackers can take American or other hostages, but for the sake of "saving human life," they advance all kinds of demands on the victims as if they were the culprits. Fundamentalist students can wreck havoc on public order in the Israeli-administered territories, but when they are arrested, "academic freedom" is invoked. In every case of this sort, which ends in a gain to the Muslims, actual or psychological, the fundamentalists score points: they have dared and they have succeeded, which means that they have to dare more, etc.

In October 1982, the Saudis sponsored an International Conference on the Islamic Criminal Justice System, where the papers read by learned Saudi scholars purported to show how Islamic law is just, fair, humane, etc., in order to assuage public furor in the West over some executions of criminals ("the Death of a Princess"). Several Muslim student associations based in North America have more recently disseminated similar messages throughout the continent. Said a tract of an association of this sort, based in Indianapolis (no date):

> Islam is a word that means peace, purity, acceptance and commitment. Islam teaches the sanctity of the human personality and confers equal rights upon all without any distinction of race or sex....The Law of God, enunciated by the Qur'an and exemplified by the life of the Prophet, is supreme in all cases.

Another tract, under the heading "Islam's Natural Appeal," states in no uncertain terms that "Islam is a solution for all problems of life," and that "Islam is the solution for modern problems." The text of the "appeal" is quite ingenious:

> A major problem which the modern man faces is racism. Materially advanced nations can send man to the moon but they cannot stop man from hating and fighting his fellow man. Islam, over the last 1,400 years has shown in practice how racism can be ended....The secular, the religious, the scientific and the spiritual seem to be in conflict. Islam puts an end to this conflict and brings harmony to man's vision of life.

Among the authors recommended to the readers of the tract were: Sayyid Qutb (the Muslim Brother who was executed by Nasser in 1966), Mawdudi (the Pakistani fundamentalist), and the autobiography of Malcolm X. Similarly, in an interview given to a Western journal (*Middle East Insight,* July 1985), Sheikh Fadlallah, one of the major fundamentalist leaders of the Shi'ites in Lebanon, spoke thus on Islam:

> Islam has nothing to do with confessional fanaticism. It is a philosophy and an ideology which is to supersede any other existing ideologies. It has room for everything and everyone, including those who espouse opposing ideologies. It is not fanatical....Islam has rules and regulations for coexistence. Accordingly, no one has the right to impose his will upon another, except in a righteous manner....In some circumstances, people have the right to impose their will on others, but Islam regulates how it can happen. What is important is that man is free....We, therefore, oppose colonialism, because it robs man of his freedom....We oppose all oppressive regimes and oppressive leaders, because we believe in justice for all people, including sinners....We believe in the liberty of man and the struggle for liberty.

Those words, which sound almost like a nineteenth century liberal manifesto, were uttered by the sheikh under a huge portrait of Ayatollah Khomeini, his hero. To the sheikh's credit it must be said, however, that he was completely honest with regard to Israel. He declared:

> Israel has no legitimate right to exist, therefore I consider that it has no right of security....We will not recognize Israel under any circumstances. It is contrary to Islam....You cannot as a Muslim say that stealing somebody's land is righteous.

Conclusion

The current wave of Islamic resurgence, whether termed fundamentalist or otherwise, is neither an aberration nor an isolated phenomenon. It is a reassertion of Islamic norms, in various degrees of emphasis, pace and aggressiveness, as it is a universal tremor that is bound to create upheaval in the world of Islam for some years to come. In Pakistan, President Zia-ul-haq enacted major measures establishing the puritanical code of Islam as the law of the land. He set up prayer rooms in factories and considered how to introduce interest-free banking and to allow non-Muslim minorities to vote only for candidates of their own religion, thus assuring continued Muslim control of his Parliament. In Malaysia, Muslim demands are mounting to make Islamic standards of conduct the law of the land. Disturbances are occasionally reported of fundamentalist elements who desecrate Hindu temples in the country. During the Lebanese War, spontaneous eruptions of Muslims and Muslim associations throughout Malaysia voiced their support for the PLO and condemned Israel and the U.S. Some even began enrolling to go as volunteers to fight on the Muslim side. The Malaysian Television reported those demonstrations against the background of Muslim prayers and Islamic religious lessons that were broadcast in connection with the Ramadan festival (July 1982). In Indonesia, Muslim extremists, who openly defy the Pancasila (The Five Principles of Modern Indonesia), are connected with explosions of banks, bombings of department stores and attacks on Christian buildings and Chinese property. Even the ancient cultural landmarks such as the Borobodor Temple complex and the Solo royal palace in Java were sacked (*Wall Street Journal*, 28 July 1985). In Egypt, the writings of the Ibn Taymiyya, the fourteenth century fundamentalist theologian, are said to be among the favorite with youth. Minorities of Muslims are also undergoing this upheaval. In Thailand, Muslims along the Malay border have been, for more than a decade, posing a serious threat to the Bangkok authorities. Even the Turkish *gastarbeiter* in Europe seem to have been touched by fundamentalism. A whole network of tape-recorded sermons and other fundamentalist writings are springing out of Germany and distributed throughout the continent. Similarly, France has growing difficulties coming to grips with its 3-million-strong Muslim community, elements of which are evincing fundamentalist propensities.

The authorities in the Islamic countries involved seem to be at a loss about controlling the resurgence of Islam, for they cannot clamp down too harshly lest their "godless" regimes become even more unpopular with the masses. They give in some and hold back some, hoping that by walking the tightrope they will be able to keep their regimes intact. Most of them seem to ignore the half-way-measure syndrome, which had brought about the Shah's and Sadat's demise: either clamp down ruthlessly, or give in all the way. Half-way measures only incite stronger appetites for more. The populace, however, seems to be swept up by the new manifestations of Islamic power and success, and continues to demand more Islam whenever Islam attains a high profile in their societies. In this regard, the people represent the "genes" of Islam, the latent impulse for re-Islamizing, while the establishment (including the religious one) represents the restraining environment.

Admittedly, the actively fundamentalistic groups in these countries are apparently in the minority, but they have behind them the silent majority of the fundamentally Muslim people who either had remained impervious to Western ideas beneath their thin veneer of modernity, or had Westernized but became disenchanted and therefore went back to the good old familiar Islam. It is these people, and not necessarily only the poor and the dispossessed, who provide the fertile ground for the diffusion of fundamentalism. It is over the souls of that majority that the authorities compete with the fundamentalists, but both, paradoxically, produce more Islam in the final analysis. On the one hand, we hear the state-controlled media of Saudi Arabia extolling their "feat" of sending one member of the royal family into space, thus creating, in their words, "the impetus for Muslims to revive the medieval glory of Islamic science," implying that the Saudi family is creating the proper environment for the revival of Islam's past glory; but on the other hand, fundamentalists in Egypt and elsewhere cite Sayyid Qutb's saying that the rule of man over man means *Jahiliyya* (The Pre-Islamic Era of Ignorance), for that implies subservience to man rather than to Allah, and denotes the rejection of divinity and the adulation of mortals. It is incumbent upon every true Muslim, therefore, to reject man's rule and find shelter in Allah's law.

However, it is not enough to cleanse the inner Islamic environments and purge them from the detrimental increments of innovations. One has also to be concerned about pursuing the elimination of the poisoning influence of the West, where *Jahiliyya* is at its apex: individualism, hedonism, sexual misconduct, dissolution of the family unit, crime and social disintegration, urban degeneration and corruption of the young. The smaller the world becomes, the more insidious the pace and intensity of the Western debilitating encroachment on the values of Islam. Hence, the urgent need for a radical change, through an inner purgatory process, to rid the Islamic environment of Western ideas and institute the dominion of Allah by the imposition of the Shari'a, the holistic code of law which embraces all aspects of life. Muslim regimes who resist this sort of change have to be fought against by means of *jihad*, and a violent one if necessary. The Saudi meek message that the splendor of Islam will be retrieved through space technology, itself borrowed from the West, appeals much less to fundamentalists than the call for the use of the sword, if necessary, to attain the same goal, faster and more thoroughly. The priorities are well ordered: first conquer the enemy nearest to you, that is internally or in adjoining Muslim countries, then go on to succor Jerusalem and the Holy Land (did Khomeini not declare that the road to Jerusalem goes via Baghdad?), and then the world lay wide open before the believers.

Notes

* An earlier version of this chapter was presented as a paper at the International Conference on Fundamentalist Islam held at Harvard University, October 13-15, 1985.

Chapter 3

THE ROLE OF ISLAM IN PRESIDENT SADAT'S THOUGHT*

Egyptian President Anwar Sadat was a profoundly religious man, and one wonders if and to what extent his Islamic background and upbringing affected his political thinking and behavior. This question has gained interest, not to say urgency, in light of the current situation in the Islamic world. While some Muslim countries have taken a fundamentalist course, the rulers of the rest of the Islamic world have been apprehensive of the "Iranian syndrome," lest the rising tide of Muslim revival submerge them as it did the Shah. In which of these two directions does Egypt face? Are Sadat's acts of signing a peace treaty and normalizing Egypt's relations with Israel likely to affect his country's path towards one course or the other?

I

Looking at Sadat's speeches and other public utterances, one is impressed by his frequent repetition of such words as "Allah," the "Prophet," the "Qur'an," "faith," "believers," "Islam" and their derivatives,[1] not to speak of the matter-of-course *"Bismillah"* ("In the name of Allah" — an opening formula before any statement by pious Muslims) at the opening of his addresses, and his citations from the Qur'an at their conclusion. Other Muslim rulers may observe the same ritual, but in Sadat's case there seems to be a genuine impulse to express his religious zeal in this fashion.

By Sadat's own account, his thought had been cast in an Islamic mold since youth. He related with admiration and nostalgia his recollections of the *imam* who taught him how to memorize the Qur'an, and he ascribed to this exercise his oratory powers and his facility for speaking without notes. Moreover, when Sadat talked of his commitment to Islam and of the need to revert to the traditions and values of the countryside,[2] he meant, inter alia, the Islamic values that he absorbed in his boyhood. He could not be clearer on this score: "Our people has a heritage of seven or eight thousand years. It confronted many invaders, but it never lost its personality....This people has manifested faith, the faith founded on the belief that Allah exists, that He is omnipotent and that we are His creatures."[3]

Elsewhere, Sadat stated:

We have faced what we can term a retreat [*ridda*] from the values we had treasured during our long and ancient history....This Homeland has always believed, and shall continue to believe, in the Divine Mission....It had recognized Truth....It is oriented to Allah and carries the Holy Scriptures. This Homeland has always been one of the most solid bastions in defense of religion, both before and after the advent of Islam....Moreover, religion has been for us, throughout generations, a vehicle of our nationalism.[4]

To his people Sadat once fervently preached:

We all believe in our Creator....We shall not abandon the Land that has produced us, we shall preserve its honor from desecration....Allah has ordained us to believe. We all need to fill our hearts with faith, in addition to the weapons we are carrying....Thus we shall enter the battle with faith...so that we may match the standard of responsibility and of the Mission that Allah has ordained.[5]

True to that spirit, Sadat, as president, promoted the role of Islam in his policies. Not only did he participate personally in such religious festivities as the Birthday of the Prophet, but in 1976 he established a special committee to recommend legal reforms designed to restore the traditional Islamic penalties against drinking liquor and of severing the right hand of thieves. It may well be that Sadat revived these laws under pressure to compete with the fanatic Qaddafi, who addressed the Egyptian masses in Islamic terminology over the heads of their leaders, or because Egypt was bound to conform to its fundamentalist Saudi benefactors. There is, however, no doubt as to Sadat's personal devotion to Islam, indicated by his condemnation of Nasser's rule as a "reign of materialism and atheism."[6]

Furthermore, Sadat stated:

After October 6 [1973], a great change was ushered [into the armed forces]....There is no question that the slogan "Freedom, Socialism and Unity" is still valid...and it will remain part of our basic principles. However, the slogan "Allah Akbar!" has become our *cri de guerre*, reflecting the change in the spiritual make-up of our troops.[7]

And, in the same vein:

I welcome the resurgence of Islamic orthodoxy that has gathered momentum in Egypt this past year and was brought home to most Egyptians when the Parliament passed last May a law banning drinking in public places....I will approve the law although it was watered down to allow sales and drinking of liquor in private and in tourist establishments. It is quite logical that in public places a Muslim should refrain from drinking liquor. We have the official religion of Islam. It is in our Constitution....We should return to the main principles of our heritage. I do not want the next generation to become a lost generation like we see in Europe and the U.S. In time of rapid change and technological development, as Egypt is certain to experience in the years ahead, a firm culture and value system will be essential.[8]

Thus Sadat's only compunction regarding this law was that it was "watered down" not to his liking. Nevertheless, he would approve such laws, perhaps in order to appear to be freeing religion from political *diktats*, whose influence he had lamented in his argument with the Libyans in 1974:

With regard to Islamic Law, our Constitution states clearly that it is the foundation of our legislation. No one quarrels with the assumption that we ought to act according to Islamic Law. The problem is that in the past fourteen generations of Islamic history Islamic Law was given to interpretations by each particular generation. At times of political deterioration, these interpretations were subordinated to *diktats* of political rulers.[9]

49

Despite his unquestionable commitment to Islam, Sadat's thought was marked by tension between blind obedience to the faith and the realistic demands of modernity. Sadat was as fervently devoted to science and technology as he was to Islam, the two being combined in his vision of the "State of Science and Faith." In Sadat's view, coexistence is warranted between the science of the twentieth century and the faith that has been rooted in the Egyptian people since time immemorial. Egypt is an Islamic country, to be sure, but if it does not open up to modern technology as a means to self-strengthening, it may lose its ability to defend itself and its faith and may even forfeit its position as the "bastion of Islam." Thus, plans for development have to be made, although Allah's will shall ultimately prevail. Once, when questioned in this regard, Sadat responded with equanimity: "As for our plans, in the coming 5-6 years, you know that we are Muslim, first of all, and we believe in Allah's Will."[10]

Though resigned to what Allah determines, Sadat realized that Herculean efforts are needed in order to change the existing reality. *"Aide toi et Dieu t'aidera"* thus becomes the moral imperative:

> Hence my request that you be attached to the same one family which knows its values and believes in Allah. Allah has willed that our life be honorable, and we must follow this course; for, if we do, Allah will be with us. On October 6 [1973] Allah's presence hovered over us. Each of us fulfilled his duties.[11]

The October 1973 "Great Crossing," an act of human will *par excellence*, brought God's presence into the midst of the fighter-believers.

Sadat, though a strict observer of the Five Pillars of Islam, did not hesitate to put aside religious practice in order to meet the requirements of modern warfare, especially when the occasion involved a "holy war." Thus, during the October War, he ordered his troops to renounce the Ramadan fast in order to ensure their full physical capacity when the crossing was launched. Sadat himself has related that at headquarters on the first day of the war he noticed that, despite his orders, the generals were abstaining from smoking and drinking because of the fast. He asked someone to fetch his pipe from his car and began smoking and drinking tea, thus signalling to the others to follow suit. Likewise, to cite another example, although Islam prohibits usury, since a modern banking system is a prerequi-

site for investment and financing, foreigners can be asked to under-
take it. Thus Sadat invited his "personal friend" David Rockefeller,
among others, to open a branch of the Chase Manhattan Bank in
Cairo.

Although science and technology were among Sadat's foremost
obsessions, he realized that they have shortcomings, unless they are
balanced by faith. In fact, Sadat had emphasized many times that the
most advanced nations have the highest suicide rates, because of
their weakened faith and spiritual values. Thus, only if Egypt revives
and preserves its countryside traditions, which are rooted in the
Egyptian, Arab and Islamic heritages, can it make the best use of
modern technology without degenerating, like other nations, into
dependence on computers and machines. Computers, Sadat remarked,
have never won a war, a claim for which the case of Vietnam
provides the best substantiation. If Egypt had calculated matters
solely in scientific terms, many of its achievements would have been
impossible. Who would have believed, for example, that the July 23
Revolution or the May 15 Corrective Revolution or the October War
could succeed? If computers had been fed with the data then available, the odds would have appeared so overwhelmingly unfavorable
as to discourage the planners from undertaking those momentous
events. Faith and inner spiritual strength were required in order to
disregard the hard facts and expert evaluations and thus achieve the
seemingly unfeasible and attain the unattainable. Sadat's frequent
references to certain "miracles" (the "miracle of October," the "miracle
of the crossing," the "miracle of the Israeli collapse") reflected his
metaphysical conception of a "military power imbued with faith."

II

Sadat not only was dedicated to Islam in the pursuit of his
domestic policies, but also was aware of the potency of the universal
umma in international affairs in general and in the Arab-Israeli
conflict in particular. He acknowledged that Islam has played a role
in Egyptian policy-making since Nasser's time, when the "Islamic
Circle" was counted as one of the "three circles" in Nasser's *Philosophy of the Revolution.*[12] During his term as the secretary of the
Islamic Congress in the 1950s, Sadat acquired first-hand experience
of the corporate power of Islam as an international force. He trav-

elled throughout the Muslim world, from Morocco to Indonesia, and must have been exhilarated by the masses of believers whom he saw and by the enormous power they represented.

Thus, when Sadat took over the presidency in late 1970, he was prone to follow in Nasser's footsteps by putting international Islam to the service of the conflict with Israel. Early in 1971, he made a statement in this regard at the International Conference of Islamic Studies, which had convened in Cairo:

> You have convened this Conference at a critical point, not only in Egyptian history, but in the history of the Islamic Nation everywhere. This country has always resolutely stood in defense of Islam and of the Islamic Holy Places. This country will remain a solid stronghold in defense of the sanctity of Islam, however cruel the sacrifices prove to be....
>
> Islam was and still is important to the Revolution....We Muslims have suffered for centuries the drawbacks of backwardness. Today, we ought to wage war against backwardness the way we are waging war against Zionism and Imperialism....We are bound to build the Islamic state on scientific foundations which will leave ample room for faith....We have to use all the scientific elements we can....Allah's Messenger had advised us to act thus, and our Faith has ordained us the same....The war we are waging these days is the war we have learned about in the Qur'an. This is a war between justice and injustice, a war between good and evil....
>
> We are entering the battle to pay the price, whatever it may be....We are not afraid of this price, and we have no hesitation about it, with the help of Allah....May Allah allow our next Conference to convene during the celebrations of our victory.[13]

On the first Birthday of the Prophet after Sadat had become president, he used the occasion to rally the faithful around him in his coming war against Israel:

> In the name of Allah, may prayer and peace rest upon the most Honorable of Messengers....In this battle that we are waging, we are required to provide ourselves with every weapon possible....As I had told you before, Muhammad and his Mission had supplied us with the most potent weapon — Faith. In history, our country

had been subjected to the yoke of conquerors and invaders, but it has never surrendered to anyone. Our people has always ultimately had the upper hand, even though it possessed no weapon other than faith....Under Muhammad's Mission, the Arab Nation was born and a culture was created....All this came about when Muhammad gathered the scattered and warring tribes to turn them into the Nation of the Faith, the Nation of the Mission....We have learned a lesson from Muhammad. In the course of history, whenever Arabs unified, they created their culture and occupied their place among nations; but, when they disunited, they were humiliated and they opened an inviting breach to foreigners and Imperialists.[14]

In this fashion, Egyptians and Arabs were called upon to stand fast as Muslims, as followers of Muhammad's example, in the face of the Israeli menace. The precedent of the Prophet was used by Sadat on the next Birthday of the Prophet to launch a vitriolic attack against Jews and Israel:

This is a period of mighty trial, first and foremost for our Faith, the Faith of the Mission of the Prophet. We find ourselves in the most difficult ordeal that we could face in our lives. They want to shatter our faith. A psychological warfare is being waged against us that claims that we cannot stand up to the Israelis and must submit to them....They all forget...that we are the standard-bearers of the Mission of Muhammad. They forgot that Muhammad and his family were imprisoned for years, yet did not submit. They made every effort to deflect him from the aim of his Mission, but he remained steadfast....

Israel, the U.S. and the like forget that we cling to that very same faith. We carry on the Mission and pursue its purpose today....We believe that Allah is on our side....We believe, as commanded by Allah, that we are a nation elected above all nations. We believe what Allah bade us in His Book, that only those with patience and great good fortune will prevail....We are preparing at present with all we have and with all our might to enter upon the glorious campaign. This is the fate awaiting us. This is our destiny and we have to fight for it....There are some who think that they can bargain, that they can conduct negotiations about Jerusalem, but Jerusalem is not in anyone's ownership, it is the property of us all, the property of the Islamic Nation....Nobody can decide the fate of Jerusalem. We shall retake it with the help of Allah out of the hands of those of whom the Qur'an has said: "It was written of them that they shall be demeaned and made wretched." Since when have these people had virtue? Only after the forces of Imperialism put themselves behind them....

They now talk of conducting negotiations. They were the neighbors of the Prophet at Medina...and he negotiated with them and reached an agreement with them. But in the end they proved that they were men of deceit and treachery since they concluded a treaty with his enemies so as to strike him in Medina and to attack him from within. The most splendid thing that the Prophet Muhammad did was to drive them out of the whole Arabian Peninsula. That is what Muhammad, the Messenger of Allah, did. We shall never conduct direct negotiations with them. We know our history and their history with the Prophet at Medina. They are a nation of liars and traitors, contrivers of plots, a people born for deeds of treachery....

I promise you that at the next Birthday we shall celebrate in this place not only the liberation of our country but also the defeat of Israeli arrogance and rampaging, so that they shall return to be as the Qur'an said of them: "condemned to humiliation and misery."...We shall send them to their former state.[15]

Referring to incontestable Islamic history, Sadat used the Qur'an to teach his audience of Muslims about the nature of the Jews and, consequently, the basis of his policies. Despite his protestations that he was not anti-Jewish, only opposed to Israel and Zionism, he unwittingly constructed a bridge connecting contemporary Israelis with the ancient Jews. Exactly as the Jews of Medina were "men of deceit and treachery," so are modern Zionists. Just as they betrayed the Prophet and thereby proved that it had been pointless to negotiate with them, so there is no use talking to them today. Moreover, if today's Muslims are the standard-bearers of the Prophet's Mission, they are bound to evict the Jews from their present location, exactly as the Prophet did. If this could be accomplished and Jerusalem could be recovered from the hands of the Jews, the Muslims will have achieved a splendid feat, again precisely as the Prophet did. Then the Jews could be returned to their former state, as *dhimmi* people

("People of the Book," i.e., Scriptuaries, such as Jews and Christians, who are protected people) under Islamic rule, the only status they deserve.

This vituperative interpretation of Jewish history was occasioned, one might surmise, by Sadat's political frustration at the time due to the hopelessness of Israeli withdrawal from Arab territories. However, even after the "October Victory," which was accompanied by a mood of exhilaration, he did not relent in his efforts to harness the Islamic world to the Egyptian and Arab cause. In his speech at the Lahore Islamic Summit, he called upon the 600 million Muslims throughout the world to show their muscle and stand behind the Arab struggle — indeed, the struggle of all believers — against Israel.[16] On that occasion, he again invoked his tie of brotherhood with all Muslims and summoned them to strive for unity in order to deal jointly with the Palestinian problem.[17] In fact, since Islam has become a success story in the contemporary world, owing to the blessing of Allah, who has bestowed oil and capital on Islamic lands, Sadat certainly felt reinforced at that international gathering, not only as the "Hero of October," but also as the leader of all Arabs and as one of the chosen sons of Islam.

III

In view of Sadat's November 1977 peace initiative, the ensuing Camp David Agreement (September 1978) and the Peace Treaty with Israel (March 1979), he seemed to have renounced, in one stroke, his anti-Israel and anti-Jewish vehemence. Moreover, in the same stroke Sadat parted ways with his fellow Arabs and Muslims, with whom he had shared his views and sought unity. What happened? Had Jerusalem and the other Arab/Muslim territories become insignificant, or had the Jews and Israelis shed their inherent wickedness? Had Sadat, as a pragmatist and realist, simply submitted to a reality that he could not change, "accepting his fate" or "taking his fate into his own hands," as he often said? Or was there a Machiavellian plot behind all this?

Judging from Sadat's insistence that Arab territories in general and Jerusalem in particular should eventually revert to Arab/Muslim rule, one is struck by the Islamic element underlying his insistence. Sadat reiterated all along that Arab lands were "sacred" and that no

Muslim (or Christian) would ever consent to Israeli-Jewish sovereignty over Islamic Jerusalem. This belief stems from the traditional Muslim differentiation between the Abode of Islam, the Realm of the Believers, and the Territory of War, which is dominated — in theory, only temporarily — by the unfaithful.

President Sadat and his close entourage not only have never renounced their obligation to abide by this Islamic worldview, but they also have missed no opportunity to reaffirm it. However, while Vice Premier Tuhami spoke of "a million Muslims who would march to Jerusalem" if it was not surrendered to Islamic rule, and other Egyptian officials have talked about the crucial issue of Jerusalem in negotiations with Israel, Sadat was much more subtle. He stated many times that his basic concept was no different than that of his fellow Arabs; he too adhered to the decisions of the Rabat Summit Conference, where the objectives of restoring the rights of the Palestinians and regaining all Arab territories became the two pillars of Arab strategy. However, since the Arabs' repeated use of force had failed either to achieve these goals or to drive a wedge between Israel and the U.S., it became essential for the Arabs to seek new paths.

In fact, Sadat argued, his broad vision had produced results, unlike the myopic view of the Arab Rejectionist leaders. The U.S. no longer favored Israel one-sidedly; and, solely by his powers of diplomacy, without spilling one drop of blood or shooting one bullet, he achieved an agreement on the restoration of his "sacred" territory, to the last inch. Similar achievements could be attained by the other Arabs, Sadat contended, if they would yield to reality and negotiate with Israel — "wretched and treacherous" though it may be — instead of persisting in their negative stance. Thus his brand of *jihad* is preferable to theirs, inasmuch as it has attained the goals sought by all Arabs, without a resort to violence. As the leader of Egypt, Sadat argued, he was obliged to conclude the best deal possible in his generation, even at the cost of normalizing relations with Israel. As for the ultimate relationship between the Jewish entity and the Arab Middle East, that can be resolved by future generations. These considerations, far from detracting from Sadat's honesty and commitment to peace, underline his personal courage and statesmanship, in that he was prepared to act against the all-Arab and all-Muslim consensus in order to reach an agreement that he regards not only as worth the effort but also as a model for a comprehensive settlement between Israel and the other Arabs. Sadat neither discarded his traditional Islamic view of the Jews nor demanded that other Arabs and Muslims do so. He merely appealed to them to change their tactics, to bend without breaking in the face of international reality. After all, what Israel is getting in return for its territorial concessions — recognition and normalization — are not irrevocable measures. Sadat expressed his distress at the failure of other Arab leaders to comprehend the basics of world politics and at their insistence that the cost he was paying was prohibitive.

Sadat's distress, however, did not stem only from his apparent infringement of the Arab/Muslim anti-Israel consensus, which had reduced him — the pan-Arab of yesteryear — to the status of pariah, but also from domestic pressures. To be sure, the Islamic establishment in Egypt is tame and can be recruited to justify either war or peace, according to the political decision of the incumbent leader. But the sweeping resurgence of Islam throughout the world has been in evidence in Egypt too, as explained above.

The driving force behind this trend is the Muslim Brothers, which has coupled its rejection of modernization, technology and Western manners in general with a stern demand that Shari'a law (the Holy Law of Islam) be restored. Banned and persecuted during the Nasser era, the Muslim Brothers came back into the open under Sadat and has been allowed to air anti-Jewish and anti-Israel sentiments, based on Islamic tradition. Their *da'wa* (religious preaching), which apparently has been well received by the Egyptian public, includes the call to rescue the entire Abode of Islam, thereby terminating the existence of Israel. This summons obviously runs counter to Sadat's peace initiative, which the Muslim Brothers rejected without reservation. Yet, unlike Nasser, Sadat did not move decisively against them (and perhaps was not able to) because of his own religious convictions and his oft-repeated commitment to the same tenets of Islam and to the need to revert to the Islamic heritage, as demanded by the Brothers.

Sadat could live with this dilemma only as long as he could point to obvious benefits from peace with Israel. If his drive for modernization had succeeded and he could show a correlation between prosperity and the peace settlement, perhaps the anti-Jewish sentiment pervasive in Egyptian/Muslim society could recede or be expediently held in abeyance. However, if the extremely high expectations of the Egyptian masses were not met and if the peace treaty was exposed as a failure, falling back on Islam as a source of comfort would only exacerbate the existing anti-Jewish and anti-Israel feelings, as happened in Khomeini's Iran. Under such circumstances, Sadat's successors either will have to return to the fold of Islam, not only on the declaratory level but also in terms of anti-Israel policies, or will be washed away, as was the Shah. It is not surprising, therefore, that opponents of Sadat's peace initiative likened him to the deposed Shah.

Hosni Mubarak, who took over upon the assassination of Sadat in October 1981, faces the same dilemmas today. His policy alternates between mass arrests and oppression of the fundamentalists, and attempts to placate their wrath by yielding to them on unimportant issues. Already alarmed by the Algerian and Jordanian examples, where democratization has occasioned the eruption of grass-roots fundamentalism, Mubarak has learned to walk the tightrope in order to survive.

Notes

* A previous version of this chapter appeared in the *Jerusalem Journal of International Relations*, Vol. 4, No. 4 (1980).

1. For a quantitative impression of the use of these terms, see the Index to Raphael Israeli, *The Public Diary of President Sadat*, 3 vols. (Leiden: Brill, 1978-79).

2. E.g., in his address at Alexandria University on the occasion of Revolution Day, Radio Cairo, 26 July 1976.

3. Address to the Arab Socialist Union, Middle East News Agency (MENA) and *Al-Akhbar* (Cairo), 25 May 1971.

4. Address to the People's Council, Radio Cairo, 28 December 1972.

5. Radio Cairo, 11 January 1971.

6. I. Altman, "Islamic Movements in Egypt," *Jerusalem Quarterly*, No. 10 (Winter 1979): 87-88.

7. Interview to *Al-Nahar* (Beirut). Cited by MENA, Cairo, 7 September 1974.

8. Interview to the *Christian Science Monitor*, 2 July 1976.

9. Message to the chairman and members of the Revolutionary Council of Libya, 7 May 1974.

10. Interview to *Ittala'at* (Teheran), 12 June 1976. Cited by MENA, Cairo, 12 June 1976.

11. Address to tribal notables in the Western Desert, 14 August 1975. Radio Cairo of that date.

12. Interview to a Yugoslav newspaper, 27 May 1973. Cited by MENA, Cairo, of that date.

13. Address to the Second International Conference of Islamic Studies, held in Cairo, in *Sawt al-Arab* (Cairo), 4 April 1971.

14. Address at al-Hussein Mosque, Cairo. Radio Cairo, 6 May 1971.

15. Address at al-Hussein Mosque, Radio Cairo, 25 April 1972. The text given here was taken, with minor alterations, from the Introduction of D.F. Green, *Arab Theologians on Jews and Israel* (Geneva: Editions de l'Avenir, 1974).

16. Arab News Agency, Damascus, 23 February 1974.

17. MENA, Cairo, 22 February 1974.

PART II: ISLAM VERSUS THE JEWS AND ISRAEL

Chapter 4

THE IMPACT OF ISLAMIC FUNDAMENTALISM ON THE ARAB-ISRAELI CONFLICT*

The Islamization of the Arab-Israeli Conflict

Part and parcel of the rising profile of Islam in the Middle East and in the world has been Islamization of the Arab-Israeli conflict. Islamization means injecting massive doses of Islamic symbols, ideas and values into an already difficult situation, something which has been increasing during the past decade and a half.

The process of Islamization adds a qualitative nature to the conflict. When one looks at conflicts between other nations throughout history, when conflicts are political or are about territory or some kind of other asset that can be touched or measured, then the conflict is for the most part a quantitative one. The parties can sit around the table, give and take, negotiate, concede, come to a compromise and settle matters. However, to introduce Islam is to introduce a qualitative, ideological angle which makes the conflict much more difficult to settle. Ideology that derives from a creed cannot be negotiated away.

For example, if one side is relying on certain passages of the Qur'an or some other holy writings in Islam, no one can agree to vote that verse out of the Qur'an. No parliament in the world can change that verse. Therefore the choice is whether to cite it or not. But when they do, as they are doing today in most of the Islamic world, then it makes their stance in the conflict much more difficult to change. This is the reason why the Islamization of the conflict makes it more difficult to settle.

63

The Iranian Revolutionary Model

The success of the Islamic fundamentalist revolution in Iran has had a definite spillover effect on the Arab-Israeli conflict, providing a model which many Palestinians have been striving to emulate. In doing so, many have embraced Islam. As a result, more and more Islamic elements have been injected into the conflict, making an already difficult problem even harder to solve. In the case of Iran, the leader of the revolution was not even present when it happened. One cannot imagine the Russian Revolution without Lenin on the scene, or the Chinese Revolution without Mao present. Yet Khomeini was living in the suburbs of Paris while his followers led the revolution. Only when it succeeded was he invited in as the hero. He recorded his message on cassettes which were listened to very carefully by the masses. Two million people went into the streets of Teheran, defying the armies of the Shah. The same type of people were seen in Hama, Syria, fighting against the Baa'th regime, and are even found in Egypt. They do not need leadership on the scene or even a call from the outside. The seeds of revolution are right there in their religion.

During the intifada some young Palestinians were caught in Nablus distributing leaflets with pictures of Khomeini. He is not even an Arab. On the contrary, the Arabs are at odds with the Iranians, and he is a Shi'ite and the Palestinians are Sunni. Nevertheless, for them he has become a symbol of someone who after 300 years of imperialist exploitation, conquest, and trampling upon the Muslim state and the Muslim people, finally came forth as a leader, someone who stood up to the Americans, who took hostages with impunity. So Khomeini has become a hero and the caption under his picture on the leaflet read: "If it succeeds there, then why not here [in the territories]?" That message has a tremendous echo in the hearts and minds of the masses, even in pre-1967 Israel. In Umm al-Fahm, Kfar Kassim and other areas, there is a rising phenomenon of that sort. It has a different nuance than in the administered territories, but it is there and we should not pretend that it does not exist.

What Do the Arabs Really Think?

When researching the image of Israel in the Arab media,[1] this author studied a cross section of the Arabic press from Morocco to

Iraq to see what they were saying about Israel after the peace treaty with Egypt. The findings are rather unsettling.

First, they say that viewed in Islamic terms, the Jews are not a nation. If they are not a nation, they do not deserve a state. In order to support that idea they offer citations from the Qur'an and other holy books in order to claim that since Judaism is only a faith, the Jews are condemned to remain dispersed among the various nations. An echo of this view can be found in the Palestinian Charter which says in no uncertain terms that Jews are only followers of a creed, whereas the Palestinians are a nation and therefore deserve a state in Palestine.

They say that exactly as there are American Jews and German Jews and French Jews, there are Arab Jews too. For Israelis this is a contradiction in terms, but for the Arabs it makes perfect sense. In this context, we can better comprehend the invitation that was heard a few years ago from the heads of some Arab states — the king of Morocco, the president of Iraq, the president of Egypt — to the Jews originating from those countries, inviting them to return.

Every Friday morning at 11 o'clock, one can hear live radio broadcasts from the mosques of the surrounding Arab capitals, including the sermons delivered by the *imam*. Usually those sermons are delivered in the presence of the heads of state. The announcer will report, "King Hussein just walked in and he is among the participants." So the sermon being broadcast is not by some obscure *imam* speaking in private. It is usually sanctioned by the state or by the head of state.

What the *imams* are actually saying is almost indescribable. They heap vicious libel and scorn not on Zionists or Israelis, but on Jews, resorting to those quotations from the Qur'an about the struggle between the Prophet and the Jews. They do not consider this an historical event that happened 1300 years ago and therefore is of no relevance today. They are continuing to manipulate this story as a very powerful vehicle to carry a political message. Anyone who understands Arabic can tune in and listen for himself or herself. It is a very useful exercise, even if it is a depressing one.

Another grievance that the Muslims advance is that Jews not only do not deserve a state, but that they have also illicitly drawn to them in Israel the Jews who used to live happily and on equal terms under the wings of Islam. But if this were so, then why did the Jews leave the Arab countries once the State of Israel was established?

Why did they not choose to remain in the Islamic paradise? And if they left, then why did they go to the State of Israel, the arch-enemy of Islam? Therefore, only the dissolution of the State of Israel will remove that embarrassment for them.

Muslims are also offended by the fact that the Jews dared to fight against the elected nation of Allah. What is worse, they even dared to win and repeatedly so, despite the fact that the Arabs vastly outnumbered them. This, they say, is a deviation of history from its original channel. It was Islam that was created in a state of conquest, of expansion, of victory, and therefore they say it does not stand to reason that this miserable people who are a minority should fight against us and win. To return things to their original channel, it is necessary to somehow dissolve this troublemaker which is Israel.

The Muslims also charge that the Israelis have conquered part of the patrimony of Islam, because the land is holy to them too, but in a different way. Since it was conquered in the seventh century by the Muslims, it has indeed been almost uninterruptedly under the domination of Islam, though not always under Arabs. It was conquered by Arabs but then came the Seljuks, Mamelukes, and Ottomans who were all Muslims. That means that the land has been ordained by Allah to be part of the patrimony of Islam and that makes it holy. To give up the land, especially if it is torn away by this vile people, the Jews, is something staggering to the mind from the Islamic point of view. Therefore it is necessary to do everything possible to recover it.

They say that in the past 1300 years there was only one exception to Islamic rule — the Crusader state. In 1099 when the Kingdom of Jerusalem was established, it was a foreign ideology, Christianity, coming from Europe, which took over by force. It established agricultural settlements and military ramparts, but eventually the Arabs united under Saladin, the great Muslim (who was not an Arab, he was a Kurd who united Syria and Egypt), and then the Muslims literally squeezed the Crusaders from Palestine. It took close to 200 years, but they believe that history is on their side.

The Jews, the Zionists, are exactly the same thing — an ideology which came to this part of the world from Europe, took it by force, established agriculture and military ramparts. So when the Arabs unite, of course they will do exactly as Saladin did. They find the similarity exact. One of the greatest champions of this analogy, before he came to Jerusalem, was President Sadat. He repeated it endlessly in his speeches, writings and interviews.

In the Qur'an there are many passages favorable toward the Jews. It is true that the Prophet said they are the People of the Book and that they received the Promised Land from God. But these are only half-truths because after the Prophet broke with the Jews he had other revelations that are very contemptuous of the Jews and those by far predominate in the Qur'an. Significantly, never in the last 100 years has one of those favorable passages been used by any Muslim leader, be it religious or political, unless to justify their political views in the West. Islam has also developed a theological way to settle such apparent contradictions in the Qur'an. Muslim theologians have developed a law of abrogation which says that all the later revelations repeal the earlier ones whenever there is a contradiction. Since it is the earlier ones that are favorable toward the Jews, they are theologically abrogated by the later ones.

The Importance of Jerusalem

A final grievance of major importance is the question of Jerusalem. The leaders of Israel as well as those in the Western world are vastly underestimating the importance of Jerusalem from the Islamic point of view. Everyone tends to discount this problem, believing it can be deferred and then settled somehow at the end of negotiations. The problem is that there is no Arab or Muslim leader who would be prepared to give up Jerusalem. For the Muslims, Jerusalem is of major significance on the symbolic level because according to their own tradition it is connected with the personal biography of the Prophet Mohammad. According to Islamic history, the Prophet Mohammad made a mysterious nighttime journey from Mecca, his native city, to Jerusalem on horseback. He tied his horse near the Wailing Wall and from there ascended to heaven. He saw the angels and then returned and rode his horse back to Mecca. That makes the Temple Mount a holy place for the Muslims.

We can ask why the Muslims need Jerusalem. Islam was born in Arabia. They have their own holy cities of Mecca and Medina. Islam is a religion by the Arabs in Arabic for the Arabs. Jerusalem had always been beyond the purview of the Prophet Mohammad. We know historically that he could not have been there. Nevertheless we have to take it seriously because in order to gain credibility, especially at its beginning, Islam had to somehow send its founder to heaven or give him some kind of divinity. Judaic tradition has the events at Mount Sinai where Moses received the Tablets of the Law from the Lord. In Christianity, Jesus Christ became the "son of God." In Islam they also wanted to somehow send the Prophet Mohammad to God to establish a divine connection. But in order to go to heaven he had to stop over in Jerusalem first, Jerusalem which was reputed to be a holy city, a city of the prophets. Therefore Jerusalem came to be incorporated into Islamic tradition. But while we may think about it as a legend, for the Muslims it is a fact of history. On the operational level, what counts is not what can be proven but rather what people believe. If people are prepared to fight and die for such things, then that is what counts.

The Jews can claim from here to eternity that they love Jerusalem more than the Muslims, but that is of no consequence to the Muslims. They will respond that they are one billion, while the Jews are 12 or 13 million. It is true that they have two other holy cities, but Jerusalem is holy for them too. They also claim that Islam should substitute for both Judaism and Christianity because it is the most updated message. Therefore there is no point in attempting to argue the matter in terms of history or archeology or proofs or evidence. The important thing is to realize how intense is their feeling.

Even the terrible war that went on between Iran and Iraq for more than seven years, longer than World War II, was rationalized in terms of the liberation of Jerusalem. None other than Khomeini, when sending his young people to the war front, stated that the road to Jerusalem goes via Baghdad. That is not only a geographical statement, which means that Baghdad is indeed halfway between Teheran and Jerusalem. It also means that once the Iranians remove Iraqi President Saddam Hussein, they are halfway to achieving the ultimate goal — Jerusalem.

In March 1979, one month after Khomeini took over in Iran and more than three full years before the Israeli incursion into Lebanon, Iran announced that it was sending a contingent of volunteers to help the Lebanese fight the Zionists. Israel does not even have a common border with Iran and the Iranians are not only not Arabs, they are at odds with the Arabs; nevertheless they sent a contingent to fight the Zionists in order "to cleanse the Holy Land from the scum of the Jews."

68

Peace or Armistice with Egypt?

What are the long-term prospects for peace with Egypt? There are Israelis who come back from Cairo and say, "The Egyptians want peace, that is what my taxi driver told me." The taxi driver may be a very important source, but if one reads what they write, the books they publish in Egypt including some that justify the blood libel as a scientific finding, and what they write in their newspapers day in and day out, one begins to wonder if Israel made peace only with Sadat and not with the entire Egyptian people.

They are continuing to talk with two voices. On the one hand, there is the establishment which is interested in maintaining the peace. On the other hand, there are the professionals, the intellectuals, writers and others who determine public opinion. For example, the Association of Arab Lawyers, with headquarters in Egypt, is perhaps the only organization in the Arab world which celebrates the day of the signing of the peace treaty between Egypt and Israel. How do they celebrate it? They burn the Israeli flag in one of the main streets in Cairo.

Under Islamic law, the world is divided into the patrimony of Islam and the rest of the world against which all Muslims must theoretically wage war until it is conquered. But Islam is also a very pragmatic faith. Almost invariably in the last 3-400 years, whenever a mufti was asked, "Should we go to war?," the answer was always, "Go to war only if you are not likely to lose and thereby to humiliate Islam even more." Islam has embraced this approach since its beginning, that if they are more or less assured that they are going to win, then they should go to war to add glory to Islam. For example, in less than 100 years the Islamic empire came to encompass a territory even larger than the Roman empire at the height of its expansion. However when they tried to conquer the Byzantines, they failed because the Byzantine empire was too strong. Therefore, according to certain patterns set by the Prophet, they agreed to a ten-year armistice with the Byzantines which would be renewed every ten years as long as they could not be overcome. In theory, everything can be justified in these terms. When Islam is not strong enough to fight, then it is an armistice.

When the peace treaty between Israel and Egypt was signed, Sadat needed the sanction of some kind of religious authority in order to sell it to his public. Therefore the Sheikh of Al-Azhar, the highest authority of established Islam, made a ruling that was published in the newspapers. He said it is good to make peace with Israel because "our Prophet Mohammad also made peace at Hudhaybiyya." No one in Israel paid any attention to the meaning of Hudhaybiyya.

What is the peace at Hudhaybiyya? In the first years of Islam, the Prophet Mohammad fought a war against the people of Mecca after he had moved to Medina. They were fighting at Hudhaybiyya, a small oasis halfway between the two, and he was about to lose the battle. So Mohammad signed a ten-year armistice with the people of Mecca. Two years later, when he was strong enough, he marched on Mecca and conquered it. What the Egyptian people understood from the reference of the Sheikh to Hudhaybiyya was that "We signed with the Jews because we could not win the war, but if in some future time, in 2 years or 10 or 50, we sense that we have enough power, there is no problem." If and when the Egyptians feel they are strong enough, they will make their move, in conjunction with other Arabs or alone. There is no other way to understand the sanction of the Israel-Egypt peace treaty as similar to that of Hudhaybiyya.

These same ideas are currently circulating in the administered territories. One leaflet put out by the Islamic organization in Ramallah starts with quotations from the Qur'an and talks about "Fight them until death." We have got used to things like this. But it ends with the words: "The time of Khaybar has come." Every Muslim knows that Khaybar is a small oasis in the Arabian desert where all the Jews living there were massacred. So the time of Khaybar has come. We are living on a powder keg and what is happening in the territories today is only one indication of that. The first conclusion to draw from all this is to be strong, to be unbeatable, to be indestructible, and to be seen as such. The Muslim faith, being a pragmatic one, must come to the conclusion that by another war they will bring about another humiliation upon themselves.

Only if the Arabs conceive of Israel as united and strong is there any chance that they will come to terms with us on an armistice that may last 500 years. In an age of ascendant Islamic fundamentalism, such an armistice is the most we can presently hope to achieve.

As long as the profile of Islam remains high, it will remain difficult to reach any political accommodation. Only when this wave of Islam recedes (and this will take a long time) and the conflict becomes quantitative rather than qualitative, can a true peace settlement with the Arab world become more likely.

Notes

*	An earlier version of this chapter, itself based on a lecture given at the Jerusalem Center for Public Affairs, appeared in the *Survey of Arab Affairs* of the JCPA, 15 August 1988.

1.	See R. Israeli, *Peace is in the Eye of the Beholder* (Mouton, Amsterdam, Berlin and New York, 1987).

Chapter 5

CONTEMPORARY ARAB MEDIA ON JEWS, ISRAEL AND ZIONISM*

On purely Islamic grounds, and regardless of the political aspects of the conflict in the Middle East, the ingathering of Jews in the Holy Land and the reestablishment of modern Israel have been regarded by many Muslims in general, and Arabs in particular, as an intolerable challenge to the Muslim worldview. The reasons are clear.

The Media as Source Materials

A study of the major Arab newspapers, magazines, and radio and TV broadcasts shows the widespread attention paid to the Jews, Zionism and Israel in the Arab media and gives the reader a sense of the intensity and repetitiveness of these major themes over an extended period of time. The question arises, however, whether the mass media provide an authoritative, true and accurate reflection of Arab thinking at the grass-roots level. The answer is a resounding "no," because the media in virtually all Arab countries are controlled by the same ruling elites that wage war, and more rarely make peace; therefore, the media do not necessarily articulate the *vox populi*, even where there is one. Moreover, unlike the media in the liberal Western democracies, which purport to represent the voices and inclinations of certain constituencies, the controlled media in the Arab world are more in the nature of a tool in the hands of authoritarian rulers in order to shape and guide, rather than reflect, public opinion. For example, there is no equivalent in the West of a "Ministry of National Guidance," which we see in many Arab countries, and which usually controls the media on behalf of the ruler. This means that the authority of the ruler includes, among its main components, the right, or duty, to teach the people and direct them on what a sound policy or a righteous leader ought to be.

Conversely, opposition to the regime directs its propaganda to the public it is trying to win over, and does not necessarily purport to represent any particular segment of the population. In other words, both the ruling regime and the opposition to it are totalistic in their aims and totalitarian in their means. They do not recognize a legitimate division of opinion, nor do they give credence to shades of political views. The truth is one and indivisible, never relative, and therefore, the ruling elite as well as the opposition (be it overt or covert, operating in daylight or underground) make no secret of their ultimate goal: to convert the entire population to the sole legitimate authority which they claim to represent. In neither case is the voice of the people heard, and in neither is there any way to determine "public opinion." We can only trace and identify the information with which the rulers and their opposition strive to indoctrinate the masses.

In contemporary Egypt, for example, the mouthpiece of the Muslim Brothers is called *Da'wa*, the very same word for political propaganda that the Abbasids had adopted during their struggle against the Umayyads in the medieval Islamic world. In both cases, *Da'wa* was devised to prepare the public for overthrowing the ruling despot and for the institution of a new ruler who would vowedly inaugurate an era of redemption and bounty. In both cases, the opposition declared its desire to restore a replica of a Muslim state as it was perceived to have existed in the time of the Prophet Muhammad, namely a community in which pristine manners, equality, justice, and the worship of Allah supposedly prevailed. Thus, one should pay attention to what the Arab media say or write about the Holy Land, not only as part of their struggle against Israel, but also as one of the many expressions of the current wave of fundamentalist Islam.

The Arab media in recent years have focused their arguments surrounding the Holy Land on five major issues: the destruction of the historical link between the Jews and the Land of Israel; vilification of the Jews as such so as to delegitimize their modern claim to Israel; denigration of Zionism as a worldwide destructive movement so as to invalidate its aspirations vis-a-vis the Holy Land; condemnation of Israel for its international "lawlessness" to discredit it with world public opinion; and accusations against the Jewish state for its alleged attempts to undermine the Muslim heritage in the Holy Land, so as to pit the entire Muslim world, and hopefully some Christians too, against the very legitimacy of Israel.

The Jewish Claim to the Holy Land

The Arab media's systematic attempt to "disinherit" the Jews from the Holy Land often leads them to rewrite history, to make new "scientific discoveries," and to press their claim to their own rights to the land instead. A few citations will illustrate the point, in spite of some built-in contradictions:

The history of Palestine started with the waves of semitic-Arab peoples who immigrated from the Arabian Peninsula and settled there. Arabs have, in fact, controlled Palestine since the year 3000 B.C. Thus, "Jewish rights over Palestine" amount to falsification of history....Moreover, Arab Palestine is tightly linked with the Islamic faith, inasmuch as it was considered by the Prophet Muhammad as the Holy Land, and the first Islamic campaign of conquest was directed to Palestine. The first Muslims turned in prayer to Jerusalem, and the Prophet Muhammad personally prayed at the site of the Dome of the Rock....After the Arab conquest, a mosque was built on that location, followed by the Aqsa Mosque....Thus, after Mecca and Medina, Jerusalem is the third holiest place in Islam....So, where is the religious right of the Jews in Palestine?[1]

The Jewish people never had any historical link with Palestine, because they were merely a conglomeration of tribes of robbers who raided the peaceful Kingdom of Canaan....Canaan was occupied by force of arms under the aegis of Joshua....After the conquest, which subjected only a small part of the country, the Jews tended to assimilate into their neighbors....The Jewish Kingdom was a negligible episode on the margin of the history of Egypt, Syria, Assyria and Phoenicia.[2]

Jews have no right or title in Palestine because they are not the offspring of Abraham, Isaac and Jacob. Jacob is not Israel, and the latter is a different person who had nothing to do with the Patriarchs or the Prophets; he was the forefather of the Jews....It is a pure act of arrogance on the part of the Jews, the killers of

Prophets, to advance the claim that they are the Prophets' descendants....Oh Muslims in the East and West! We must again shatter the arrogance of the Jews, and this can be accomplished only when we unite in the cause of recovering Jerusalem! Jerusalem is Arab-Islamic, and the Messenger of Allah will not be satisfied until Jerusalem reverts to being Arab and Islamic again.[3]

Even after Sadat's peace initiative of November 1977, the Egyptian press remained adamant in its charge that the Jews had relinquished their relationship to the Holy Land, although some credibility was imputed this time to Jewish sources who claimed such a relationship. The fact that by advancing this argument Egyptian journalists pulled the carpet from underneath their leader's peace initiative, which implied recognition of Israel's possession of the Holy Land, did not seem to bother them much:

> The history of the Jews came to an end in A.D. 70. Begin has stated that the...Balfour Declaration enabled the Jews to return to their homeland and that they did not expropriate anyone's land. But the truth of the matter is that the Bible itself depicts the details of the conquest of Palestine by the Israelites and the expropriation of its owners which resulted. In fact, the Canaanites, Emorites, Philistines and the other peoples which had inhabited Palestine, never abandoned it. The Bible bears witness to the constant wars between the Israelites and the local peoples of this area. Jews, exiled to Babylonia, Assyria and Egypt, mixed and assimilated with the local population while very few responded to the Cyrus Declaration and returned to Palestine.[4]

Vilification of the Jews

Arab barrages of hatred against Israel and their vituperative condemnations of Zionism, both aimed at invalidating Jewish national aspirations in the Holy Land, are reinforced by a systematic denigration of the Jews, which feeds upon traditional Arab as well as imported European antisemitic stereotypes. A few examples will make the point:

The Jews think of themselves as particles of sand which, the more they are trampled upon, the more glittering they grow....Like grapes, when they are squeezed and stamped on, they generate wine....But beware! The Jews have turned the particles of sand into flakes of venom likely to consume the feet that step on them and the lips that kiss them; similarly, they have transformed the wine into a terrible poison for anyone who would attempt to taste it....

Jews never relent from torturing themselves and excrutiating others. No wonder they gave birth to such a man as Freud, the famous scientist of the soul, who gained a reputation as the expert on fear, horror, complexes and death; or Kafka, who was attracted to the black color, of all colors, and projected it on paper, onto all lands and onto European literature....

It appears that the Jews, by means of their printing houses, their cinemas and newspapers, have brought upon humanity all manner of suffering....They demonstrated their innate propensity for selling their inner tranquillity for money, and they substituted sex for honor and for civilization and religious values....They are the originators of revolutionary, anarchistic, communist, disruptive and deviationist ideologies, thus undermining the very society where they mean to live, injuring the very hand that was extended to help them, and wounding the hearts that pitied them.[5]

The Jews in general are treated in a derogatory manner in the Arabic press. Indeed, when the "Jewish character" is analyzed, straight antisemitic stereotypes are evoked. Jews are depicted as masters of trickery, cheating, plots and treachery, and as archenemies of Islam. The Jews are said to be loaded with psychological complexes and fears, they have a sense of inferiority to others and of imaginary suffering. They masochistically torture themselves with these feelings and sadistically force others to share them. For example, the television series "Holocaust," which the Arabs claimed was full of distortions, was calculated to "erode the conscience of Europe." The Jews were accused of being themselves the cause for their oppression by others. Other very current claims usually hurled against the Jews are their forgery of history and of their Hebrew sources, and their secretive ways which enable them to plot mischievous deeds:

The Bible is not reliable for this kind of information: we have already warned Arab authors against relying too much on stories of the Jews (*Isra'iliyyat*) where facts are distorted by the Jews at will, with a view of breaking into Arab history and sharing it....After the death of Joshua, anarchy prevailed among Hebrew tribes until the Judges ascended. These were no more than military commanders, but they were idealized in the Jewish Bible and made into mythological heroes....Archaeological findings have proved beyond doubt that the Hebrew language, which is claimed to be holy, and the Bible, which is claimed to have been given by God, were written down only during the sixth century BCE, while Moses had lived in the thirteenth century BCE, and his law had been written down in old Egyptian, 800 years prior to the advent of Jews....The Jews confuse various historical periods and chronologies of events. They meddle with history in order to credit themselves with existence well before they came into being....[6]

The Talmud is an historical scandal that the Jews try to conceal. This book is regarded as secret, therefore they do not encourage anyone to read it or translate it. Hence the importance of publishing excerpts from it, because of the hatred it reveals on the part of the Jews towards all other peoples. They believe that they can kill at will Christians and Muslims and take over their property. Whoever kills a Jew is a murderer in their view, whoever kills a Christian is not a murderer. Whoever steals from a Jew is a thief, but whoever steals from a Christian or a Muslim is no thief.[7]

Even after the peace process between Israel and Egypt began, the Egyptian press persisted in telling "personal stories" to show how mischievous, greedy and shady were the Jews.[8] Anis Mansur, perhaps the most vitriolic anti-Jewish raconteur who poses as an "expert on Jewish affairs," elaborated on this theme of Jewish greed, for example, by enjoining his readers to "just imagine who the Jews are," following his description of their burgeoning success in selling empty cans full of air from the Holy Land.[9] He explained that the first word that a newborn Jew utters is "one." "Is it to designate the oneness of God? Certainly not. The first words that he utters are simply numbers."[10] According to some Arab media, corruption and decadence are intrinsic to Jews and were transplanted with them into the Holy Land. Under the heading "The Children of Israel are bastards," a Saudi paper wrote:

> The kibbutz is a place where boys and girls live together and do not even know who their parents are. Youths engage in sexual intercourse in public, in the middle of the road, or right in the heart of the kibbutz, without any sense of shame....This is the way they continue the tradition of their bastard predecessors.[11]

Denigration of Zionism

When the Arab media talk about Zionism's vision of the Holy Land, they usually depict it in terms of an expansionist lust which pushes the boundaries of the land far beyond the present Israel. "Israel is bound to expand as a condition of her continued existence," is the motto of many Arab media. They contend that Zionism, in concert with world imperialism, provides the ideological rationale for Israeli expansion "from the Nile to the Euphrates." To their mind, Zionism is a godless creed in the grip of an insatiable greed which will not slacken until the universe is enslaved by the Jews. The Arab media also contend that, concurrent with its external imperialist aggression, Zionism conducts a policy of internal racist aggression towards its Arab and Oriental-Jewish populations. For Zionism is, in essence, a racist ideology which sustains the Jews as the master-race in the Holy Land. They claim that the racist attitudes of Zionism are anchored in such Jewish sources as the Talmud. Therefore, Zionism considers itself free to expropriate lands, to deny the Arabs their rights, and to discriminate against Oriental Jews. As a racist entity, Zionism in the Holy Land is the natural ally of the racist regime in South Africa.

So when the General Assembly of the U.N. adopted its infamous 1975 resolution condemning Zionism as a form of racism, the Arab media rushed to "explain":

> Zionism is racist because it is the religion of the Jews only. Judaism is a family religion which is transmitted by tradition. No missionary activity is practiced in Judaism, and it is extremely difficult to become Jewish or to acquire Israeli nationality....The

Jewish engineers, doctors and rabbis who have migrated to the Holy Land were constrained to import dark-skinned Jews in order to perform menial labor in Israel....In this fashion, they carried out the "Magic Carpet Operation" whereby they brought in Yemenite Jews to sweep the streets and cultivate the land....Zionism is interested in white Jews, but discrimination obtains even against white Jews from Western origin who are considered inferior as compared with white Jews from the East: the Poles and the Russians....But all these bands of Jews are considered as superior to the Arabs dwelling in Israel.[12]

One of the most recurring generalizations made by the Arab media with regard to the "racist" nature of Zionism in the Holy Land is to compare it with other racist regimes. A Jordanian newspaper predicted that a "common fate is awaiting all racist regimes, and Zionism is bound to follow in the footsteps of Rhodesia and South Africa."[13] The visit of South African Prime Minister John Vorster to Israel in 1976 was seen as a growing indication of the complicity between Zionism and *apartheid* and was dealt with accordingly. The commentator of Radio Cairo found "striking similarities" between the Vorster Government's treatment of the blacks in South Africa and Namibia, and Israel's actions against the Palestinians in the occupied territories of the Holy Land.[14] A Lebanese magazine explained that, "like South Africa, Israel has been besieged by world public opinion due to the growing international indignation at the aggressive nature of the Zionist state and the barbaric racism of South Africa"; since the UN had placed Zionism within the category of racism, the cooperation between Israel and South Africa could best be termed "an alliance of pariahs."[15] Another newspaper even expected the application of *apartheid* in Israel with Pretoria's aid, "in view of the experience accumulated in South Africa in this matter and Israel's desperate need to resort to such an experiment after its attempt to swallow up the populations of the land occupied since 1948 has dismally failed."[16]

The list of Arab accusations against Zionism also includes the following:

a) Israel confiscated Palestinian lands under the pretext of self-defense, and declared them "closed zones"; more land was expropriated under the excuse of dispersion of the population and concern for social and environmental development; Israel established garrison settlements along its 1967 borders, under the cover of kibbutzim, thus usurping even more land; the Zionist state has been harming Arab culture and perpetuating illiteracy among its Arab citizenry; Israel granted higher salaries to the Palestinian Arabs in industry than in agriculture, with a view to encouraging Arab migration from their lands and permitting the establishment of more Jewish settlements; Israel's policy towards the Arabs exposed the cancer-like expansionist trends of Zionism and its philosophy of imperialism, capitalism and colonialism.[17]

b) The Zionist state is pursuing a war of genocide against the Arabs of the Holy Land; Israel did not implement UN resolutions regarding the return of the refugees to their homes; Israel has taken over natural resources in the occupied territories, confiscating Palestinian real estate and bank accounts; Israel has been destroying Arab villages and houses in the occupied territories.[18]

c) The best proof of Israel's deeds is, of course, the pile of condemnations heaped upon it at the UN General Assembly, the Security Council and other UN agencies. The result of all this is that since the Arabs' right to defend themselves against Israel's excesses is well-established, the Arab boycott of Israel cannot be considered other than a legitimate form of self-defense.[19]

d) The change of government in Israel in May 1977, far from being seen as a manifestation of the democratic process, was on the contrary condemned in the Arab media as a further provocation to the UN, the international community, peace-loving nations, and the Arabs because "the treacherous adventurers who ascended to power in the racist Zionist entity will make more use of their war machine, supplied over the years by the U.S., under the pretext of preserving Israel's security."[20]

Israel's International Lawlessness

Perhaps the most striking instance of dissonance between the awe that the idea of the Holy Land inspires and the reality of today's Israel is found by the Arab media in the Zionist state's patterns of lawless international behavior. Israel is, indeed, regularly accused of serving the cause of imperialism, of bullying Third World countries, of scheming to take over the world or large parts thereof, of launching uncalled for attacks against innocent and powerless countries, and of collaborating in those Satanic endeavors with the darkest forces of evil in the world. The inference is clear: to counter the danger that Israel allegedly poses to the world, an internationally-concerted effort is required. Let us listen to some of these voices:

> What has been published in recent weeks about the Straights of Bab-al-Mandab goes to the root of the Jewish ambition to dominate the Arab countries. In the past, Jews hatched plans to turn the Red Sea into a Jewish lake, to serve them as their second base [after the Holy Land] to launch their two-fold long-term plan: to set up the Greater Jewish state...and to expand into African and Asian countries with a view of controlling their markets and natural resources.[21]

> Israel is well aware of the importance of the Third World to her economic and political schemes; therefore, she invests great efforts beyond the diplomatic relations she maintains there in order to deepen her penetration....Israel has stood behind the 23 coups which took place in 14 African states during the years 1963-8....Israel's penetration into these countries was facilitated by world imperialism which harnessed all developing countries to its benefit....In any case, Israel's aid to the Third World does not amount to 25 percent of what Israel gets in indemnities for the Jews of World War II....Israel takes advantage of the shortage in skilled manpower in these countries in order to dump her own experts and training programs there....Although not much can be done [to check Israel's inroads], political factors have of late limited and weakened Israeli influence in the Third World, mainly due to her aggressive and racist policies.[22]

"Proof" of Israel's designs against the Third World could be seen by the Arab media not only in the "proverbial cooperation between Israel and the racist regimes of Rhodesia and South Africa,"[23] but also in Israel's intervention in the affairs of other countries, and in it "plans" to conquer the oil wells of the Arabs.[24] The tension between Ethiopia and the Sudan at the beginning of 1977, for example, was thus interpreted by a Syrian newspaper:

The Ethiopian regime has lost its prestige in Africa....The Ethiopian regime has been playing an imperialistic role as a proxy of imperialism and Zionism, which are historically linked together....Israel is always ready to push the Ethiopian regime towards confrontation with African Arabs, as a link in the Zionist-Imperialist conspiracy.[25]

Along the same lines, Israel's commando operation in Entebbe, Uganda, in July 1976, to rescue hijacked hostages, was viewed by the Arab media as a flagrant violation by Israel of the sovereignty of Uganda as well as a threat to all Africa. Here are some examples of these views:

Rhodesia and South Africa were satisfied at the success of the Israeli operation because the West and its extension in Israel have regained their military superiority, thus putting an end to the illusion of equality among nations and to the domination of the UN by the developing countries....The most serious repercussion of the Israeli raid lies in the pressure that it exerts upon the relationship between rich and poor nations, precisely when the latter have decided to open consultations establishing a new world order.[26]

No matter how much the Zionists and their supporters strive to endow this act of piracy with glorious heroism, they are only proving once again that nothing deters them from operating like gangsters, from adopting fascist and criminal methods, and that they are the enemies not only of the Arab people but of all African, Third World and free people of the world.[27]

Israel's operation in Entebbe is reminiscent of the barbaric onslaughts which civilization has undergone throughout history. Moreover, it brings to mind the laws of the jungle....Israel's very base is aggression and its history is sown with acts of aggression...such as the abduction of Eichmann from Argentina which generated international wrath against Israel for its violation of territorial sovereignty....Israel's operations are those of professional criminals, international gangsters and sworn terrorists....One ought to confine those vile beasts in the jungle rather than let them run wild and inflict military, political and economic chaos throughout the world.[28]

The Arabs must understand that Israel is the main virus of piracy which is apt to suck blood and slaughter innocent victims....Israel has sought to intimidate the African peoples and to please the racists of Rhodesia and South Africa, in order to strengthen the legend of the white man's superiority....Only Golda Meir's sons are capable of such an act of cowardice.[29]

According to the Arab media, Israel's political, military and economic conspiracy to corrupt the world order is matched only by an equally perverse plot in the moral domain. Israel is also accused of extorting money, indulging in moral excesses, in line with the innate qualities of the Jews, and engaging in organized crime and international espionage. The Arab media insist that these "illicit acts" are as indicative of Israel's decadent nature as of her meddlings in the international arena:

The lie of the murder of six million Jews by Nazi Germany has served as a pretext to the Zionists to extort money from the German people, and it is a continuing excuse for further extortion....Since 1967, the Zionist authorities have attracted to Israel 10,000 young Germans who volunteered for work in the kibbutzim....During the three-month period of volunteer work, the German youth were subjected to oppressive and humiliating treatment, insults and physical beatings on the part of the Zionists, both within the kibbutzim and in the streets of the cities....More than 1,500 German girls, who volunteered for work, were pressured into responding to the approaches of the Zionists. These young German girls were forced into prostitution in the cities, and their earnings went to kibbutzim treasuries. In addition, these young girls were compelled to satisfy the sexual lust of the kibbutz members.[30]

Arab embassies abroad employ many British secretaries....These secretaries, regardless of whether they are efficient in their jobs or not, ought to be kept under surveillance because most of them are either Zionists or serve as agents of the Zionist racists....We have prohibited our Arab diplomats from marrying foreigners...so how can we put up with employing these secretaries and giving them access to our offices and official papers?[31]

Desecration of Holy Sites

By far, the most outrageous effect of Israel's presence in the Holy Land is, as far as the Arab media are concerned, its domination of the Muslim Holy Places. For this fact is related in Arab minds with the contention that Jews are bent upon the destruction of the Islamic heritage in general and the Islamic institutions of the occupied territories in particular. This contention is centered by the Arab media upon what they see as the obvious physical evidence of the desecration of the holy mosques in Jerusalem and elsewhere. Indeed, the argument is advanced that the Israeli excavations close to the mosques have been undertaken with the specific intent of undermining the mosques' foundations and causing their collapse, so that the Jews can reconstruct their Temple on the site. This applies equally to the 1969 arson of the Aqsa Mosque, which was perpetrated by an Australian tourist, but for the Arabs this was, all the same, yet another attempt at "judaizing Arab lands and destroying the holy places of Islam."[32]

Nothing can better illustrate the fervor with which Israel's devilish designs against Islam are perceived by the Arab media than their annual commemoration of the Aqsa arson. Eight years after the event, Arab newspapers wrote:

When the Zionist enemy set fire to the Aqsa Mosque, it intended to hurt the feelings of the Arabs during the most difficult moment of their defeat...ignoring the anticipated furious reactions of the Islamic world....If the enemy has not yet reached the stage of trembling with fear from the Muslims, then the convening of the Islamic conferences will ultimately bring about Islamic solidarity and the recovery of Jerusalem into Islamic hands.[33]

It has been eight years since the Zionist occupying forces set fire to al-Aqsa Mosque, in the framework of a well-calculated scheme to...annihilate the Islamic heritage and place the Holy Sites under Zionist control. This act of provocation, which offended the sentiments of the Islamic world and constituted a blow to international law, was designed to alter the status of Jerusalem.

The occupying authorities are also pursuing their digs around the Aqsa Mosque, thus posing a threat to its foundations....The Israelis who entered [into the Mosque] through the gates of the city, used to perform dancing parties while in a state of drunkenness, and at the same time other groups attacked Muslims who prayed, in an attempt to hold their parties within the mosques....Because of the resistance of the Arabs in the face of these attempts, the Israeli authorities were forced to expose their criminal face as they set fire to the Mosque on August 21, 1969....

Israel committed the same sort of crime against the Church of the Nativity on March 29, 1971, when an Israeli entered the church, chased the visitors and began wrecking havoc and destruction on the Holy Tomb. He attacked the priests....Israel has tried ever since to cover up the story.[34]

The Jews are further accused of attacking mosques throughout the territories under their occupation in the Holy Land, of molesting Muslim worshipers, of breaking into holy places and of tearing up copies of the Holy Qur'an. The Israeli court system is charged with legitimizing such acts by allowing Jews to penetrate and pray in Muslim houses of prayer. Jews are also found guilty of destroying Arab houses adjoining the Western Wall, and of confiscating lands with a view of taking over the property of the Waqf (Muslim charitable trust). Israel is accused of building new neighborhoods and even an Olympic center to obliterate the holy and Islamic character of Jerusalem. Desecration of the tombs of the prophets and of Christian sites, such as the Holy Sepulcher, is similarly imputed to Israel. The indictment of the Jews and Judaism is thus a corollary to the charges laid at Israel's door regarding her antagonism to Islam. Indeed, Jews are viewed as the eternal enemies of Islam since the dawn of history. In the period just preceding Sadat's journey to Jerusalem in 1977, the Arab media, in general, and the Egyptian press, in particular, were replete with scholarly responsa by Muslim *ulama*, passing derogatory judgment on the Jewish faith and its Scriptures. Jews were accused of having assisted such enemies of Islam as the Byzantine and Sassanid empires, and of having made false and perverse arguments against the faith of Islam. The conclusions, of course, were that the Jewish self-ascription to the Patriarchs having been falsified, Jews have no part in the Holy Land, nor can they lay claim to the Western Wall. A few samples will suffice to give an idea of these accusations:

> Following the 1967 War, Israeli officers broke into the Tomb of the Patriarchs, accompanied by 50 girls, and performed sexual intercourse on the site. These are the Children of Israel, those bastards who claim to be the Chosen People.[35]

> The Zionist enemy has stolen valuables from the Tomb of the Patriarchs. The local population detected the abominable crime when they visited the tombs following the lifting of the curfew....In Hebron and the Arab areas, resentment has been building on account of this terrible crime by the occupying forces.[36]

> The materialist-atheist Zionists are still awaiting the fall of Islam and the Muslims, and they are spreading their poison by means of false slogans, distorted arguments and religious plots. Only the unity of Islam in *jihad* is likely to generate success.[37]

> Anyone who visits Jerusalem under the shadow of the Israeli occupation cannot help noticing the scandalous contempt shown by the Israelis towards all the holy places in the city. People enter the Dome of the Rock building with glasses of wine, girls behave extravagantly....The Church of the Holy Sepulcher has been robbed...and many buildings which surrounded the Wall have been torn down in order to accommodate more lamenters in the area of the Wall.[38]

While practically all Arab media called for a *jihad* to liberate the Temple Mount from the perversity of the Jews, who are the enemies of Allah and of humanity, and who stand behind all the conspiracies and corruption of the world,[39] an Arab newspaper gave a ray of hope for Jews, if they could only shed Zionism from their system of beliefs:

> The Temple Mount has a God and a people to defend it....The Arab people consider Muslim, Christian and also Jewish holy sites as national monuments, and they will defend the Temple Mount from any fanatic who might try to desecrate it....After liberation is achieved, all Zionists should be excluded from the

Wall; Jews would be allowed access only if they dissociate themselves from Zionism.[40]

Although the Arab media charged Israel with desecrating the holiness of the Holy Land in general, their special attention was understandably centered on Jerusalem. Some of the arguments they advanced included:

a) Jerusalem was holier to Muslims than to either Christians or Jews, for Jesus Christ was born in Bethlehem and reared in Nazareth; his vicars, the popes, have established their seat in Rome. Jerusalem had been the capital of the Jews, but only for a brief period of 100 years, during the reigns of David and Solomon, after which the Jews split into two kingdoms and Jerusalem was the capital of only one of them.

b) To Islam, Jerusalem had a special meaning which was incorporated in its Arabic name — Al Quds (the Holy). This implied sanctity and a deep reverence on the part of Muslims, and Muslim activity in this city has always reflected its particular religious import.

c) Allah has given to the city many of the Prophets of Islam, headed by Abraham, the Father of all Prophets, and down to Jesus Christ.

d) The ascension of the Prophet to Heaven had taken place from Jerusalem.

e) Jerusalem had been the first direction of prayer (*Qibla*) for all Muslims, and it houses their third most important mosque.

f) Jerusalem is the city of the revival of the dead. Islamic sources confer much importance on it, and on prayer within its confines.

g) Jerusalem has always been Arab. Since Islam and Arabism are inexorably intertwined, anything that is proved Arab is also, by definition, of importance to Islam.[41]

Conclusions

Palestine as the Holy Land figures prominently in contemporary Arab media, but much more so in the wake of particular events which seem to the Arabs as threatening their own interpretation or concept of holiness. Thus, Jerusalem and Hebron could exist, under Muslim rule, as backwaters of the West Bank of Jordan during the nineteen years of Hashemite rule. But as soon as they fell into Israeli hands, their sanctity came to the fore as an overriding concern for all Arabs and Muslims as never before. We have also seen that the Aqsa Mosque arson, and the melee at the Tomb of the Patriarchs in Hebron, were used by the Arab media as a lever to condemn anything and everything the Israelis were doing in the territories that came under their rule in 1967, including archaeological excavations, building and development, new settlements, services to the population, intervention to excise antisemitic passages from school textbooks, etc.

In the intervals between these anti-Israeli and anti-Jewish outbursts, which have religious as well as political roots, the Arab media hammer in the message, day in and day out, that the present occupants of the Holy Land, namely the Israelis (or the Zionists, in Arab parlance), have lost whatever claim they may have entertained in its regard. For as Jews, they are godless forgers of history and falsifiers of facts; as Zionists, they are racist and they cultivate aggressive and destructive designs; as Israelis, they are outlaws who plot all manner of schemes, and pursue perverse and corrupt policies. Under these circumstances, even if they had a legitimate claim to the Holy Land, they have forfeited it. For a holy land, so to speak, cannot bear the desecration and rampage allegedly wrought by Israel. Moreover, the Jews' fallacious claim to the Holy Land has been superseded by the rightful and righteous title of the Arabs to it. For them, as for other Muslims, the land is not only holy due to the many holy places to Islam that it contains, but also due to its central position in the heart of Islamic history and in the focus of the Abode of Islam.

Delegitimizing Israel's hold on the Holy Land, by condemning its regime, denigrating its movement of national liberation and vilifying its people, has thus become for the Arabs a favorite way of advancing their own claim to it. The logic of holiness goes even further than that: in order to rescue the Holy Land from its vile usurpers, it is not only permissible, but indeed required, to wage against them a *jihad*, a holy war. To retrieve the Holy Land through the Holy War — that is the purgatory process that will render to it its despoiled holiness. And when holiness is recovered, the profane people who had discredited it — the Jews — will have no part in it.

These themes and more, which are rooted in Islamic tradition, but have also extensively borrowed from European antisemitism, gain more or less prominence in the Arab media depending on the fortunes of the Arab-Israeli conflict. While in the aftermath of the Israeli-Egyptian peace treaty there was a lull in the Egyptian press in addressing these issues, the Lebanese war, the Taba dispute, and then the intifada again brought out the worst of the Arab, including Egyptian, innate anti-Jewish sentiment. A few examples will illustrate the point:

> These Zionist gangs constitute the trash of the nations of Eastern Europe....This riff-raff claims that they are the descendants of Abraham our father, and they link themselves to him with an impudence that generates disgust....The documents of the "Masonite" Zionist Protocols are the greatest world conspiracy against humanity....We see complete correspondence between the content of the Protocols and their plans, and the content of the Jewish Torah and Talmud.[42]

Even when Zionism is not specifically mentioned, the Jews are attacked by the Arab press:

> Because they denied God, Allah has caused the Jews to be hated among humanity, and everywhere on the face of the earth. Because they lied and spread falsehood against Allah and humanity, Allah struck them with the decree of destitution and misery, and in fury they were removed from him.[43]

Saudi officials, too, have on occasion openly resorted to vituperative antisemitic language. Thus, at a UN Seminar in Geneva (5 December 1984) on the Encouragement of Understanding, Tolerance, and Respect in Matters Relating to Freedom of Religion or Belief, Saudi representative Ma'ruf Dawalibi said, among other things:

> Why did Nebuchadnezzar expel and scatter them [the Jews] throughout the world? Why did Hitler want to exterminate them?...It is because they call themselves the chosen people and allege that they were chosen by God from among all the other peoples....What has brought oppression of the Jewish world from these ancient times to this very day is their belief.

In Egypt, after its peace treaty with Israel, Jews and Israel are slandered in the harshest language:

> Israeli society is a racist society, hostile to other religions....The Jews claim that...other peoples are merely creatures who may be killed and slaughtered, whose blood may be shed and used for baking matzoth for the holidays of the Jews.[44]

> Zionism has a written constitution and its name is the Talmud....[The Talmud] contains a call upon Jews to corrupt the world with sex, drugs, and infiltration, the mixing of races while maintaining the cleanliness of the Jewish race, the imposing of an iron hand on the economy of the world and the media in order to press them into the service of Zionism, which is simply total control of the world.[45]

The rising tide of Islamic fundamentalism around the world in general, and in the Middle East, Israel and Israeli-held territories in particular, has provided yet another outlet for Arab-Muslim antisemitism. The platform of the Hamas movement, a sister organization of the Muslim Brothers in the administered territories, unabashedly states in its seventh article:

> Allah's Messenger already spoke of a time when the Muslims would fight the Jews and kill them, and the Jews would hide behind rocks and trees. The rocks and trees say: "O Muslim servant of Allah, this Jew is hiding behind me, come and kill him." Only one bush, the wild orache, is an exception to this rule because it is a Jewish bush.

The Jews are accused by Hamas of controlling the world's wealth and media, of instigating revolutions and of setting up clandestine organizations such as the Freemasons, Rotary and Lions Clubs, B'nai B'rith, etc., which engage in espionage and destruction and concoct world wars in order to take over the world (Article 22). Virulent antisemitic statements of this sort are also found in cassettes distributed by the Islamic movement in the territories and are repeated in its public announcements related to the intifada. As noted earlier, one of them explicitly stated that "The time of Khaybar has come," implying that exactly as the Prophet had conquered that oasis in Arabia, massacred some of its Jews and subjugated the rest, it was time to act likewise vis-a-vis the present-day Jews of Israel.

The importance of these statements lies in the comprehensiveness, totality and vituperative tone of their negation of Jews and Israel. What is more, unlike PLO political statements, which are man-made and therefore are theoretically amendable, the Hamas platform, which is backed by extensive quotations from the Holy Qur'an, creates the impression of reflecting universal, eternal and Allah-given truths that are immutable and unalterable. It is this added dimension of Islamic fundamentalism, which is incremental to the traditional anti-Jewish sentiment among the Arabs, which has lent to the Arab-Israeli conflict a qualitative emphasis which makes it all the more intractable.

Notes

*   This chapter was presented as a paper at the International Conference on Judaism and the World, Johannesburg, Fall 1988.

1. *Jaysh al-Sha'b*, 19 October 1976, p. 16.

2. *Al-Ba'th*, 8 November 1976. See also 11-19 November.

3. *Al-Akhbar*, 15 August 1977.

4. *October*, 22 November 1977.

5. *Akher Sa'a*, 3 December 1975, pp. 5-8.

6. *Al-Ba'th*, 8 November 1976. See also 11-19 November.

7. *October*, 5 June 1977.

8. See, e.g., *October*, 25 December 1977.

9. *October*, 25 December 1977.

10. *Al-Ahram*, 28 December 1977.

11. *Al-'Ukaz*, 20 February 1976.

12. *Akher Sa'a*, 3 December 1975, pp. 5-8.

13. *Al-Dustur*, 7 November 1976.

14. Radio Cairo, 21 February 1977. See also Radio Damascus, 21 February 1977.

15. *Al-Hawadith*, 16 April 1976.

16. *Al-Ra'y*, 5 April 1976.

17. *Al-Baa'th*, 29 March 1977.

18. *Al-Anwar*, 26 July 1977.

19. *Ibid.*

20. *Tishrin*, June 1977.

21. *Al-Dustur*, 9 January 1977. See also 12 and 17 January.

22. *Al-Ra'y*, 5 April 1976.

23. Radio Cairo, 7 March 1977.

24. *Akher-Sa'a*, 21 July 1976.

25. *Al-Baa'th*, 14 January 1977.

26. *Al-Thawra*, 6 July 1976. See also Iraqi News Agency, 5 July 1976.

27. *Al-Gumhuriyya*, 6 July 1976. See also Middle East News Agency (MENA), 4 July 1976.

28. Radio Cairo, 6 July 1976.

29. Radio Damascus (Palestine Corner), 4 July 1976.

30. *Al-Fajr al-Jadid*, 29 July 1976.

31. *Al-Thawra*, 21 June 1976.

32. See, for example, MENA, 7 March 1977.

33. *Al-Madinah*, 22 August 1977.

34. MENA, 21 August 1977.

35. *Al-Ukaz*, 20 February 1976.

36. Jordanian News Agency, 28 October 1976. See also *Al-Urdunn*, 8 October 1976; *Akhbar al-Usbu'*, 7 October 1976; MENA, 4 October 1976; Radio Damascus, 15 October 1976; and Radio Amman, 3 October 1976.

37. Sheikh al-Azhar, as quoted by MENA, 30 December 1976. See also *Al-Akhbar*, 4 March 1976; and *Al-Dustur*, 1 March 1976.

38. *Akher Sa'a*, 5 February 1976.

39. See, e.g., *Al-Ra'y*, 15 March 1976; Radio Amman, 19 March 1976.

40. Palestine Radio, Lebanon, 8 February 1976.

41. *Al-Gumhuriyya*, 11 April 1978.

42. *Al-Watan* (Kuwait), 2 September 1988.

43. *Al-Riyadh* (Saudi Arabia), 21 November 1988.

44. *Roz Al-Yousouf*, 6 August 1987.

45. *Al-Akhbar*, 26 December 1987.

Chapter 6

UMM AL-FAHM: THE HEART OF FUNDAMENTALIST ISLAM IN ISRAEL*

In the mayoral elections of February 1989, the Islamic movement in Israel made its first major impact through democratic means. Umm al-Fahm, the largest Muslim town in Israel and the long-standing pioneer of Islamic revival among the Israeli Arabs, elected at its head a predominantly Muslim Council led by Sheikh Ra'id Mahajneh. This impressive young leader, who successfully combines religious knowledge with political charisma, probably exemplifies the trend of Islamic fundamentalist involvement in politics. How he emerged, how he unseated the previous Council led by the Communist Rakah Party, which had dominated the scene during the previous elections, and how he is lending a novel configuration to Islamic politics within a local council, are the questions to be examined in this chapter.

The Setting

Umm al-Fahm was the largest Arab village in Israel until it reached a population of 25,000, which lent to it the municipal status of a town. Its name means the "mother of coal," probably relating to the times when the local inhabitants would cut the trees in the adjoining forests and manufacture coal. The town lay at the foot of Mount Emir, or Ras Iskandar, a 350-foot hill which overlooks the Jezreel Valley. It is the central settlement in the Ara or Iron Valley (Nahal Iron), a fertile and narrow lowland which connects between the coastal plain of Israel to the west and the Jezreel Valley to the east. Umm al-Fahm is but one of a string of Arab villages located in the same valley, the most important of which are Ara, Ar'ara and Baqa al-Gharbiyya, another major center of the Islamic movement and a traditional rival of Umm al-Fahm as the commercial and cultural center of the valley. The strategic importance of the valley and its population centers goes back to Pharaonic times, when it

95

served as a vital artery for Egyptian troops on their way to nearby Meggido. In 1918, when British troops took over the Holy Land from the Turks, they used the Ara Valley to break through Turkish lines into the Jezreel Valley and from there to the Galilee. In the 1948 War, Iraqi expeditionary troops held positions along the strategic valley and they engaged in battles against the nascent Jewish state. It was not until the Armistice Agreement with Jordan in April 1949 that the valley and its Arab villages came under Israeli rule. Since then, the Iron Valley, which harbors one of Israel's vital highways connecting its central cities to its northern districts, has become one of the key strategic areas of the country.

Umm al-Fahm encompasses a microcosm of the problems of the Arabs of Israel: once a prosperous village living on agriculture, it became an urban area depending for its livelihood mainly on neighboring towns and cities; once comfortably spread out on the slopes of the hills of Wadi Ara, it is now miserably congested by a dense array of haphazard, ill-planned and ill-maintained clusters of houses cut across by narrow alleys and unpaved roads; once tranquil, low-key, homogeneous, conservative and patriarchal, it is now bustling, multifarious, modernizing and youth-oriented; once relaxed, re-signed and easy going, one can now sense the tension, bitterness and plotting in its atmosphere; it used to be tidy when the population was manageable, now it is squalid as the population pressures and density mount; in the past, the population was diffident, conscious of its majority-turned-minority status, now it is bursting with a self-confidence born out of the self-imposed quasi-isolation from the Jewish State of Israel, out of their self-consciousness which attaches them to the vast realm of Arabs and Muslims around them, and out of their optimism that they are on the right track facing the future.

These characteristics, which are admittedly common to most Arab villages in Israel, are more salient in Umm al-Fahm not only due to the concentration of a large Arab population in a limited area, but also due to the pioneering role of this town in its support of the Muslim movement. Eighty percent of the once predominantly farming work force have become construction workers, 90 percent of them day or permanent laborers outside the village. Often, they would rather stay overnight in their place of work than commute daily back to their village. Years of Israeli military government (1948-1963) had forced these individuals to entrench themselves and seek comfort within their family and clan shelters, and so their voting patterns during elections followed family or clan lines. Tension and friction within the clans often burst out into inter-family and inter-clan rifts which further sharpened their political differences and made them rival clients seeking the protection of rival political patrons. At the same time, due to dramatic improvements in health care and the rising standard of living, the local population grew rapidly, from 5,500 in pre-1948 Palestine to some 25,000 in 1988. The population pressure, which was not matched by a parallel growth of resources, increased the misery and bitterness. Moreover, the area of land held by the inhabitants of Umm al-Fahm had allegedly shrunk from 140,000 dunam in 1948 to about 14,000 today, which illustrates the transition from a rural to an urban society. This process of de-ruralization, however, has not been superseded by a reverse process of industrialization, hence the reliance of the local work force on services and out-of-town labor.

In 1960 the first local Council was elected in Umm al-Fahm. The election campaign, as well as the composition of the Council, reflected the family and clan divisions in the village. Even the candidate of the Communists was returned by his clan votes, in spite of the seemingly "ideological" nature of his campaign. The four major clans were and still are: Ajbariyyeh, Jabbarin, Mahajneh and Mahamid. All elected members of the Council had always been identified by their constituents as their kin and they themselves built their appeal on family kinship. Lately, although family ties are still strong, most members of the Council identify along party lines. For example, the Council which preceded the February 1989 elections was made up of Communists from the predominant Rakah list, representatives of the "Sons of the Village," a radical Arab party, and the Ansar, a political group which had split from the "Sons of the Village." For about 14 years, the head of the local Council was a Rakah Communist.

Since the 1950s, and against the above-described trend of disaffection, Arab nationalism, whose champion was Egypt's President abd-al-Nasser, began seeping into the Arab population of Israel. Umm al-Fahm, the pioneer and laboratory of political innovation among Israeli Arabs, witnessed in these years the first buds of the first Arab separate (not to say, separatist) political movements. Occasionally, members of the Arab community were arrested by the Israeli security services and accused of either sabotage activities against the state or espionage activities on behalf of outside Arab powers. That was the period when the "Sons of the Village" movement was at the peak of its activity in Umm al-Fahm, which openly advocated struggle against Arabs who "collaborated with the Zionist establishment," and denounced the Israeli Arabs (namely the majority of them) who participated in the election process of Israel, thereby lending legitimacy to the Jewish state. But their impact was minor, while most Arabs elected to become part and parcel of the democratic fiber of Israel as the best avenue to attain their socio-political goals.

When one talks today to the people of Umm al-Fahm and inquires about the root reasons for the rise of the Islamic movement in the village, one is almost invariably referred to the squalid state of affairs in the streets and to the sense of helplessness and bitterness resulting therefrom. But things seem to be more complicated than that, especially in that Umm al-Fahm has been not merely *one* of the centers of Islamic revival, but the focus thereof. It appears that the universally agreed watershed was 1967 when, following the defeat of the Arabs in the Six-Day War, a paradoxical process set in throughout the Arab world: on the one hand, a deep sense of humiliation, and on the other hand, an iron-clad resolve to seek redress by identifying the illness that had affected the Arabs and then strive to find a remedy and apply it vigorously. The remedy usually prescribed by Islamic circles throughout the Arab world was the return to Islam. Moreover, the renewed encounter between Israeli Arabs and their brethren across the "green line" in the territories newly occupied by Israel lent a new impetus to this trend, insofar as feeling part of a larger whole imbued the Arabs of Israel with a new sense of confidence and optimism.

The youth of Umm al-Fahm were quick to catch up with the new wave. One of them, Sheikh Ra'id (b. 1958), went to the Islamic college in Hebron in 1976 and after graduating in 1979 he began roaming the country and professing a return to Islamic values. An Islamic organization was set up in Umm al-Fahm as in other places, complemented by voluntary welfare associations which sought to step into the social and cultural vacuum left by the lack of socio-economic involvement of the Israeli government in the village.[1] The Islamic message had a tremendous appeal to unskilled laborers who worked in Tel Aviv and underwent their daily humiliation in their encounter with Israeli prosperity and cultural assertiveness. It also appealed to youth who were seeking new directions and new answers, and to professionals who were in search of new channels for their nationalism and new definitions for their identity. The movement also appeals to the rank and file who observed with admiration and pride the welfare, development and cultural projects that the Muslim movement was undertaking in the village. As the accomplishments of the movement shone, the traditional organizations of the kinship clans and political parties were dwarfed and made irrelevant. Much like the great feat of the Prophet Muhammad thirteen centuries earlier, when he created the *umma* in which all individual Muslims could find comfort and shelter irrespective of their tribal affiliation, the new Islamic movement provided a new form of socio-economic and religio-political organization which transcended and superseded the old forms.

Opinion "Polls" and Election Votes

We conducted an unofficial "poll" in Umm al-Fahm in early 1987, where over 60 percent of the 60 polled men, women and youth vowed support to the Islamic movement in case of elections. This forecast was to be fully realized in the February 1989 elections to the local councils in Israel. A more detailed "poll" was conducted in May-June 1987 among the two top classes of the Umm al-Fahm High School, where students from adjoining villages, such as Barta'a, Ar'ara and Musmus, are also enrolled. From the scores of students only 23 responded to all or most questions and agreed to submit their questionnaires. Six of the respondents were female, the rest young men. Both the narrow sample and the social pressure not to conform make this "poll" inadequate and unreliable as a precise yardstick to measure the depth and scope of Islamic sentiment among this age group. However, it can certainly indicate a mood, a state of mind, a general direction. This assumption is born out by the fact that a similar "poll" conducted among Arab students at Hebrew University yielded much the same "indications" (though certainly not "results").

These are the questions, which were written in Arabic, and in which the students were not asked to identify themselves, but only mention their gender, school, grade, age, village of residence and the name of their school. The replies are categorized into male and female students, and they consist of multi-choice answers in which the respondents could choose one or more possibilities (a-f). Due to the multiple choice, it is understood that the aggregate number of answers exceeds the total number of questions.

Q-1 Did you notice a return to religion in your village?

A-1 Most students agreed that there was a *widespread* (7 males and 3 females) or *medium* (6 males and 2 females) movement of return to Islam. A small number (4 males and one female) noticed only a *slight* reversion to Islam, and no respondent claimed that he/she had noticed no Islamic movement of this sort.

Q-2 What are, in your opinion, the reasons for this return to Islam?

A-2 Most male students (10) but a minority of the females (1) claimed that the main reason is *social*. Fewer male students (6) but more females (3) diagnosed the reason as *political*. A minority of students believed that the reason was *economic* (3 males, no females). Others thought that the return was due to *concealment or cover up* (2 males and one female), and 3 males believed that return to Islam was done for *"personal interest."*

Q-3 How do you place yourself vis-a-vis the Islamic movement?

A-3 Most male students (10) declared that they were *supporters* of the movement, only one identified himself as *activist*, two had *reservations* about it, but only one *objected* to it. Four stated their *neutrality* (indifference) toward it. Among the female students one regarded herself as *active*, two as *supporters*, none *took reservation* or *opposed*, and four (the majority) were *neutral*.

Q-4 Those who stated that they were *active* (an overall minority) were requested to specify the nature of their activism in terms of the time they devoted to the movement. Understandably, most respondents did not write down any answer.

A-4 Two males (no female) answered that they devoted *10 percent of their time*, four males (no female) committed *20 percent of their time*, two males and two females gave *50 percent of their time,* and three males gave the movement *70 percent of their time.*

Q-5 Does the movement represent only Muslim youth or others too?

A-5 Most males (9) and females (4) believe that the movement represented *all social milieus* in the village. A small minority (2 males and 1 female) thought that it represented *mainly the youth* of the township, and the rest (6 males and 1 female) thought that *not only the youth* was represented.

Q-6 What are, in your opinion, the goals of the Islamic movement?

A-6 Most respondents identified *religious goals* as preponderant in the movement's program (11 males and 2 females); others (7 males) stated that their goals were *social and cultural*; only a minority (3 males and 2 females) identified the goals as *political*, but an almost equal number (4 males and 2 females) believed that the goals of the movement encompassed *all those elements combined*.

Q-7 Can the movement constitute a viable option in the upcoming elections?

A-7 A slight overall majority (10 males and 2 females) thought that the Islamic Movement *could present such an option*, while a minority of 7 males and 4 females believed *that it would not*.

Q-8 Would you like to see the movement participating in the upcoming local elections, or the general elections, or both?

A-8 Six males and 4 females stated their wish to see the movement participate in *both elections*, while 5 males and 2 females *rejected both*. Another group of 4 males wished the movement's participation in the *local municipal elections only,* while 2 males opted for *general elections only*.

Q-9 Is the Islamic movement a unifying or a disuniting factor among the Arab sector in Israel?

A-9 An overwhelming majority of 13 males and 3 females thought it was *uniting*, and a minority of 4 males and 1 female thought it was *disuniting*.

Q-10 Did you personally notice the activities of the movement in your town?

A-10 A majority of 8 males and 3 females noticed *widescale* activity; an almost equal number (7 males and 2 females) noticed only *slight* activity, and a minority of 2 males and 1 female noticed *no activity*.

Q-11 In what domains did this activity manifest itself?

A-11 Most participants (14 males and 5 females) noticed *religious* activity; a somewhat similar number (10 males and 3 females) noticed *educational* activity; for 11 males and one female noticeable activity was in the *social* domain; and only 3 males and 3 females were aware of *political* activity.

Thus, social and sex differences notwithstanding, the majority of the "polled" youth in the township of Umm al-Fahm, apparently reflecting the general mood in their families and their environment, thought that the Islamic movement, in all its manifestations, was evident and gaining ground. Even without a poll, one could gather that evidence all across Arab society in Israel: dozens of new mosques are springing up in the Arab villages in the Galilee and the Triangle, where Umm al-Fahm is located; groups and associations are sprouting, oriented towards Islamic activity; and there is even an amazing Islamization (not Arabization) of sports clubs. For example, in soccer, an "Islamic League" of 42 clubs has been established, representing Arab villages in the Galilee and the Triangle, separate from the all-Israel leagues where individual Arab-Muslim players are members of Israeli teams, and all-Arab teams compete for their standing in the general weekly games. The only difference is that the Islamic League teams kneel on the soccer field before each game and fervently recite their prayers, imploring Allah to impart victory to their team.

The February 1989 Elections — The Ascendance of Sheikh Ra'id

The municipal elections of February 1989 signalled to the Israeli public, in general, and the Arab-Islamic sector, in particular, that the Islamic movement had turned from a socio-cultural pursuit for born-again Muslims into a religio-political organization which seeks power as a way to implement its program. Indeed, while in the 1983 elections only one Muslim movement mayor had been elected together with 6 councilmen in 4 different Arab villages, in February 1989, 5 Muslim movement mayors were elected, together with 45 other councilmen in various municipalities and local councils. Hence the "watershed" mood in many Arab local councils where, depending on one's political loyalty, one either feels confident and euphoric or fearful that the upswing of Islam has begun.

Judging from the overall gains of the Islamic movement in the local councils where they stood for election, their success in the Triangle, where Umm al-Fahm is located, was over 30 percent of the votes (25 out of 81 councilmen), as compared with 15 percent in the Galilee (8 out of 52) and 23 percent in the Negev (3 out of 13). However, compared to the total number of councilmen in the Muslim villages in Israel (396), in most of which it did not run, the Islamic movement's overall score is just over 10 percent. Still, looking at the entire Triangle, the Muslim movement elected 25 out of the 116 councilmen — 21.5 percent.[2] This comparatively high percentage can be accounted for by the fact that, unlike the Galilee where many Christians reside, the Triangle Arab villages are almost exclusively Muslim.

What happened in Umm al-Fahm during the elections, where the slogan "Islam is the solution" (*al-Islam Huwa al-hall*) was rife, focuses on the immensely charismatic figure of Ra'id Salah Mahajneh, the founder and leader of the Islamic movement in the town and its elected mayor, who swept into City Hall with close to 75 percent of the votes and 11 out of the 15 councilmen. At the age of 30, he became the epitome of the Islamic movement's swift storming of the political scene among Israel's Arabs.

Sheikh Ra'id[3] is a member of the Mahajneh clan, a formerly Druze family in Syria which had converted to Islam, moved to Palestine, and helped found the village of Umm al-Fahm. After graduating from the local high school he studied at the Islamic College in Hebron where he was ordained as a Sheikh. In 1988 he was also awarded the prestigious title of "Haj" following his pilgrimage to Mecca. Ra'id has been the central figure of Islamic revivalism in the town throughout the 1980s, although since the 1970s a mood of return to Islam has been prevalent among the 20- and 30-year-olds, who now constitute the backbone of the local leadership and of its constituency. Due to the backward quality of the local services, and the physical degradation of the township, Sheikh Ra'id was one of the first who took the initiative into their own hands in order to show that they could do what the establishment had failed to achieve before them: he and his followers collected garbage from the streets as a model to their fellow townsmen, and he and others announced that they were contributing part of their salary to the bankrupt local treasury.

His opponents in town claim that he was swept into office not only because of twelve years of systematic *da'wa* (propaganda) that the Islamic movement had judiciously planned and executed among the population, and not only due to the social services that the movement, headed by Sheikh Ra'id, conducted for all the deprived in the town, but mainly by reason of the aggressive election campaign that the fundamentalists had devised. By spreading the slogans "Islam is the alternative," "Islam is the Truth" and "Islam is the Solution," and by lending an almost "divine" quality to their populist and hopeful platform, Ra'id's fundamentalists could present their opponents, notably Hashem Mahamid of the Rakah Communist list, as anti-religious; in effect, voting for him was made tantamount to Allah's "lese majeste."

Just prior to the elections, Ra'id was taken to court by his opponents, the Communist Party, who contended that instead of printing his full name on the voting tickets, as required by law, he contented himself with his first name, Ra'id, and his father's name, Salah. The combination "Ra'id Salah" meant "The Righteous Pioneer," a rather attractive name for the candidate of the Islamic movement. Sheikh Ra'id actually belongs to the Abu-Shaqrah clan, which just happened to settle within the Mahajneh clan's neighborhood, one of four in the township. Thus, in spite of a quirk local custom which made one's identity contingent on one's quarter of dwelling, the young sheikh rebelled against that convention because he wished to identify himself as a candidate of all the local inhabitants, not only of the Mahajneh clan, to which he belonged only technically. However, he lost his case in court and he was compelled to conform to the rule and to add his borrowed clan name to his voting slips. Nevertheless, his success was huge, and except for his opponent's clan, the Mahamids, which closed ranks behind their candidate, an overwhelming majority of the village's overall constituency voted for him.[4]

On election night, when the first returns were announced and predictions were voiced regarding Ra'id's success, he was so overwhelmed by the stunning margins that he retreated to his home and even cancelled a live TV interview. His supporters and followers were overcome with joy and shouts of victory were heard throughout the small alleys of the overgrown village. The Sheikh's house was invaded by a jubilant crowd of hundreds who came to have a glimpse at, and an occasional hug with, the triumphant but still diffident and incredulous young leader. Soon the courtyard of the house overflowed with thousands who came to greet him for his/their unexpectedly vast victory. The Sheikh had ultimately to appear before his followers and speak to them in his soft but clear voice, sprinkling his words, as is his wont, with citations from the Holy Qur'an and the *hadith* (accounts of oral traditions relating to the life of the Prophet Muhammad).

Ra'id is a preacher at heart. Whenever you ask a question, he replies with a speech. Aware of the bad experience of the 1970s, when his fellow townsmen were incarcerated because of their acts of sabotage (burning woods and crops in nearby Jewish settlements), he is now extremely cautious not to express his political views, under the pretext that all his attention would now be devoted to the pressing municipal affairs of Umm al-Fahm. He pledges to pursue the preaching of Islam without, however, resorting to coercion or force, a statement that he immediately contradicts when he affirms: "we shall not tolerate the sale of alcoholic drinks in Umm al-Fahm. If there is no municipal regulation to that effect today, we shall adopt one."[5]

Islamic Media and Islamic Rhetoric

The most important organ of the Islamic movement is *Al-Sirat*, which is edited and printed in Umm al-Fahm. *Al-Sirat* (the Path) derives its name from verse 5 of the opening chapter of the Holy Book (*al-Fatihah*) "Show Us the Straight Path" (*Al-Sirat al-Mustaqim*). The choice of "al-Sirat" not only makes sense by and in itself[6] for a Muslim revivalist movement, but its very designation also sheds light on the thinking of those who have made that choice. For the "Straight Path" appears in the Book not merely as a positive definition of the believers (in our case the members of the Islamic movement), but also as an exclusive statement towards those who do not follow the path (i.e., the Jews and the Christians). Verses 6-7 of the text are explicit: "The Path of those who earn Thine anger, nor of those who go astray."[7] Thus, *Al-Sirat* is to enlighten those who have elected the Straight Path and to perpetuate their difference from, and contradiction with, the Jews — namely, the host society amidst which they live, and the Christians, including their fellow-Arabs who share with them their minority status in Israel.

Al-Sirat is not only the major medium of the movement to spread its revivalist ideas on matters ranging from return to the faith to women and youth, but also the main platform for reacting to contemporary events and for engaging in rhetorical battles against its opponents. For long before it grew into an effective political power, the movement built its ideological base by reinforcing its followers internally and challenging its opponents externally, and seeking to rally around itself the hesitant, uncommitted, and even its foes. *Al-Sirat*, which began with a distribution of 1,500 copies in June 1986,[8] and quickly passed the 10,000 mark by the end of 1989, has been a powerful tool in propagating the Islamic movement's viewpoint. It soon bifurcated into a weekly and a monthly and became the main voice of support for the intifada.[9] Towards the end of 1989, the weekly *Al-Sirat* was supplanted by a new weekly, *Sawt al-Haqq wal-Huriyya* (The Voice of Truth and Freedom), also published in Umm al-Fahm, but the monthly *Al-Sirat* continues to appear.

The Islamic movement of Umm al-Fahm expounds its positions in other media as well, be they posters, leaflets or written messages (*risala*) worded by the head of the movement, Nimr Darwish, who follows in this regard the example of the founder of the Muslim Brothers in Egypt, Hasan al-Banna. To counter their main political foe, the Communist party (Rakah), who had accused the young adherents of the movement of being "criminals who squeeze money from the public under religious pretexts," or "collaborators and agents of the Israeli authorities," leaders of the Islamic youth group in Umm al-Fahm have occasionally used their own enemies' platforms to profess their concerns. One case in point was the unprecedented debate published in *Al-Ittihad*, the official mouthpiece of the Communist Party, which was triggered on 28 February 1989 by Salem Jubran, a Christian, and the editor of the journal. As R. Paz has pointed out,[11] Jubran undertook to attack the Muslim movement in Israel using the same approach and tools of the Egyptian left-wing intellectuals in their own confrontation with Islamic fundamentalists in Egypt. He placed the Muslim revivalists in Israel in the context of the current universal religious "reactionary wave" and pleaded with Muslims not to turn religious sentiment into a political instrument of power.

Hamed Agbariya, one of the leaders of the Islamic movement in Umm al-Fahm, countered with a rebuttal entitled "Islamic Religion is Not an Archeological Vestige to be Relegated to Museums" and published in *Al-Ittihad* of 18 March 1989.[12] Agbariya argued that exploiting religion for political objectives was not only permissible but even imperative in any Muslim society, and contended that it was Islam which cared about social justice much more than the Communist ideology invoked by Jubran. That argument has become all the more persuasive since the total collapse of Communist regimes in Eastern Europe at the end of 1989 and, conversely, the gathering strength of the Islamic movement both in Israel and in the administered territories during the intifada.

The debate between the Islamic movement and the Communist Party is conducted over the soul of the same constituency, and so far the Communists have been losing ground to the Muslim fundamentalists, as the February 1989 elections in Umm al-Fahm have shown. Up until then, the Communists purported to represent the national Palestinian sentiment among Israeli Arabs, an argument that the Islamic movement could not refute, lest it lose support among the strongly nationalist Palestinian-Arab population of Israel. Up until then, both the Islamic movement and the Communists evinced support for the PLO platform and pleaded their commitment to a Palestinian state side-by-side with Israel. In other words, in spite of the ideological obligation of the Islamic movement to their brethren in the territories, the Hamas, they had refrained from identifying with the latter's unequivocal call to substitute an Islamic state over the entire expanse of Palestine for the existing state of Israel. Moreover, as Paz has rightly shown,[13] the Islamic movement had avoided theretofore any call or insinuation of separation or autonomy for Israeli Arabs.

However, the prolongation of the intifada, in which the Hamas had been gaining prestige among the Palestinian public, on the one hand, and the tremendous success of the Islamic movement in the February 1989 elections in Israel, on the other, have apparently strengthened the hands of the more radical elements within the movement. Sheikh Darwish, the head of the movement, who represented the more conciliatory and "national" line of the Palestinians, has been apparently upstaged by the younger and more militant sheikhs who now unabashedly lend much more primacy to the Islamic factor and come dangerously closer to the Hamas line of argument. Already in late 1988, first indications of that shift were noticeable in *Al-Sirat*,[14] when an editorial stressed that "the Palestinian people have hoisted the banner of *jihad* in order to die for the sake of Allah." They quoted an eight-year-old boy who had purportedly stated to his Israeli captors that he was "acting under the order of Umar Ibn al-Khattab, Khalid Ibn al-Walid and Salah a-Din al-Ayyubi."[15] Again following the example of the Hamas, an editorial in *Al-Sirat* accused Israel of the arson of a mosque in the village of Ibtan and heaped on it the following insinuation:

Satan had advanced the claim of the superiority of his Nazi race over the human race. Now his disciples profess the superiority of a certain race over all the rest. Satan has indeed found disciples of flesh-and-blood who are implementing his doctrine faithfully. Anyone who respects himself ought to stand up against Satan and his army; the caravan of Belief alone, when united, is able to undo their schemes.[16]

That article, which was concluded by a call to "raise a strong generation, a generation of *jihad* and martyrdom," was unprecedented, inasmuch as it could be interpreted as a direct incitement to rise against Israeli rule within Israel proper, something that only the Hamas had uttered previously. Since then, and especially following the February 1989 elections with their corollary mounting of the Islamic movement's self-confidence, the call for *jihad* against Israel has become routine.[17] The November 1989 issue of the monthly *Al-Sirat* went further when it reproduced a picture of the Aqsa Mosque on the cover of the journal with the caption: "Oh fighter of *jihad*! Wake up! Acre and its shores are calling upon you! Don't fall asleep, come and defend our rivers!" Anti-Jewish elements, again following the Hamas example, creeped into the publications of the Islamic movement in the following months. In the December 1989 issue of the monthly *Al-Sirat*, there is a clear reference to the "domination of the world media" which facilitates the exploitation of world public opinion by the Jews. Denial of the Holocaust is also one of the themes of this anti-Jewish rhetoric. An article in the *Al-Sirat* weekly stated:

> Foreign visitors are taken to Yad Vashem[18] where they spill crocodile tears, which have nothing to do with truth and reality....This is part of Jewish scheming.[19]

The same issue, incidentally, also hails, in a poem, "Identity," the "future glory, when our patrimony: ...Jaffa...Jerusalem, the Triangle,[20] the Galilee, the Jezreel Valley," would be retrieved![21]

Full identification with the Hamas is no longer merely implied since April 1989, when it was explicitly stated in *Al-Sirat*:

> We cannot forget the pioneering role of the Hamas in Palestine against the forces of occupation, which are injecting the masses with the passion that would expel occupation from the Holy Land and hoist the banner of Allah.[22]

Delegations of the Islamic movement in Umm al-Fahm have rendered condolence visits to the families of the fallen during confrontations with the Israeli army in the territories.[23] In an editorial in *Al-Sirat*, the Islamic movement called upon the Arab Summit in Casablanca to do something for the martyrs of the intifada and enjoined them to remember that "the land of Palestine is an Arab and Islamic land, the property of the Arab nations and the patrimony of all generations of Muslims until Allah inherits the land and its inhabitants."[24] Moreover, a clear reference is made to the famous *hadith*[25] that is quoted in Article 7 of the Hamas Platform, to the effect that Jews will hide behind trees and rocks before the Day of Resurrection, but the rocks and trees will shout: "O Muslim, a Jew is hiding behind me, come and kill him!" The editorial in *Al-Sirat* states unequivocally:

Trees and rocks will acquire, by Allah's help, human qualities, including the capacity of speech. They will play a crucial and constructive role in the struggle against tyrannical rule, travesty of justice, disasters and the laws of the jungle [that are practiced by Israel].[26]

Al-Sirat, expectedly, hailed the victims of the intifada as heroes[27] and labelled the Israelis who fought them as "maddened dogs."[28] But, surprisingly for their usual caution not to transgress the limits of law, they began inciting for the escalation of the intifada, and, again like the Hamas, refuted all political options for settlement. Sheikh Muhammad al-Ghazali sent a message to the intifada fighters, over the pages of *Al-Sirat*, calling on them to turn their land into an "arena of *jihad* where the flame would burn continually."[29] This rhetoric, to which the Israeli authorities did not respond by legal means,[30] gathered momentum until it culminated in an editorial denying the right of Israel to exist and anticipating its destruction:

The politicians of this country pursue their vain ideas regarding the frontiers of their state from the Nile to the Euphrates. We will not be surprised if some of them will lay claim to Hijaz.[31] The very statement of this idea constitutes a Zionist invasion which was patterned after the Crusades. Their venomous arguments and their forgeries of history, far from serving their goals,

109

contribute, on the contrary, to the rule of aggression and oppression....Those lies and forgeries will not convince us to accept the *fait accompli*. All political solutions that have been proposed around us will not persuade us to renounce our ideological justice....Anyone who has behaved, for a few years, as a peasant in the land...will not be able to prove that the land is his, for his parents may have usurped that land. They forget that it was the Balfour Declaration which granted them in 1917 a national home in Palestine. That was to be a one-shot expediency which cannot be transformed all of a sudden into a national right....

You should content yourself with the fact that for the time being the world has recognized you as a nation, but you should not delude yourself any further lest you wake up to a horrible reality....Your very existence, which is based on arrogance and high-handedness, is but delusion and vanity, and therefore it is void by definition, because it is not predicated on legitimate rights and accepted truths, but upon vain premises and means of usurpation, killing, expulsions, domination of others' lands by force...and the establishment of a society of ingathered from all parts of the globe whose inner contradictions are evident....

Their arrogance is proof that they have learned nothing from history....The laws of the Universe will bring upon them a decisive rout, the like of which they had suffered at the hands of the Romans and others. They will always be parasites in other nations' civilizations, due to their obduracy and defiance of history and its laws. Their arrogance can only lead them from one defeat to another.[32]

Once that Rubicon was crossed, public appeals to Muslims in Israel "to liberate Palestine and establish in it the rule of Allah," or enjoining Muslims to "respond to the call of *jihad* quickly and willingly in order to win or die,"[33] became a matter of routine. A poem written by a member of the movement urged "the liberators of Jerusalem to trample upon the hideouts of the Tatars,"[34] and another, written by a tenth grader, Muhammad Ibrahim Jabbarin, called upon "mountains of fire to rise against the basest humans who will not be able to slaughter us forever....We, the children of stones, challenge anyone who wants to dominate us and who will end like a dead dog."[35] Others dehumanize the Israelis by telling about them all manner of unlikely horror stories connected with the intifada,[36] followed by straight-forward calls to "remove the venomous teeth of the crusader-like snakes," to "challenge the dogs who bark and display their lion muscles," and to "silence their barking with spears and knives."[37]

The announcements of the Hamas in the administered territories (numbered 1-50 by the end of 1989) are routinely and sympathetically quoted by *Al-Sirat*, in spite of their clear language of incitement against Israel, and unambiguous wishes for the success of the Hamas are cited in every issue of the journal.[38] Moreover, *Al-Sirat* proudly reported the names and pictures of three children, two from Umm al-Fahm and one from Nazareth, who had adopted "Hamas" as first names.[39] Hamas, heretofore occasionally mentioned as stated above, became the predominant factor in the stories of the intifada cited in every issue of *Al-Sirat*.[40] Concurrently, the clamor against Israel kept mounting not only with regard to the territories, but *equally* with Israel itself. Prominence was given to an interview with members of the family of a fallen Hamas member which said, inter alia, that:

> Those thieves are coming to settle on the lands of our fathers. The citrus groves which used to belong to Abu Hasan in Jaffa are now Menachem's property....The olive trees of the Galilee have been taken over by gangs of murderers and drug dealers from the back alleys of New York.[41]

All these themes and more were picked up by *Sawt al-Haqq wal-Huriyya*, which began its appearance in October 1989 as a substitute for the *Al-Sirat* weekly. Israelis, who are accused of objecting to the right of Palestinians to freedom, are dubbed "unbelievers and dogs," and the crowds are encouraged to pursue their war of rocks and other attacks against the Israelis.[42] This new journal seems, however, to surpass *Al-Sirat* in its blunt antisemitic broadsides, and there is reason to believe that its appearance in lieu of *Al-Sirat* was precisely calculated by the Islamic movement so as not to put in jeopardy the *Al-Sirat* publications (monthly and weekly) should the authorities move against the journal by legal or administrative means. Besides the usual laudatory words about the Hamas, the call to the Soviet Union to rescind "Jewish immigration to our homeland," and a renewed clamor that "liberating Palestine is a national, patriotic and

Islamic duty," *Sawt al-Haqq* proceeded to publish anti-Jewish accusations which are strikingly identical to those of the Hamas platform:

> The Israelis are on their way not only to rebuild their Temple but also to take over the world, in accordance with their historical scheme which entails that the Law of Zion shall prevail....They not only aspire to build their Temple on the ruins of the Aqsa Mosque, and to turn the Mosque and the Muslim Holy Shrines into tourist sites, museums and playgrounds, but worse — they strive to destroy Christian civilization and to establish Israel as a world dominion. There is no limit to their greed and expansionism. Some of them believe that their Messiah, based in Jerusalem, will appear under the cover of darkness like a thief, or will appear in the form of lightening, and this exemplifies their desire to rule the world.
>
> If we understand this, we are on solid ground to comprehend their megalomania. One of their sages had declared:"We, the Jews, are the destroyers and will continue to be destroyers forever. Anything you, the gentiles, would do cannot respond to our needs and demands. Therefore we shall continue to destroy forever, because we want our own world, a divine world, the like of which you are unable to construct.".
>
> They aim not only at the Temple, not at gaining Palestinian concessions nor a piece of land, for they will never be satisfied with any nation and they believe that even the very best of all nations deserve to be killed, let alone our own [Arab] nation which has shown a great deal of resistance [to their schemes]. It was an American writer who has warned the Western world against the Zionist extremists who had caused America's involvement in World War II. These same secretive forces are also likely to bring about a third world war in order to dwarf the Arab countries and make them subservient to Israel.[43]

How central is the role of Umm al-Fahm as the source of inspiration for this rhetoric is exemplified not only by the fact that it is the home of the *Sawt al-Haqq* journal, but also that it often cites the young mayor of the town, Sheikh Ra'id, one of the leading figures of the Muslim movement in Israel. In one instance he referred to an incident in which a group of Israeli fanatics had attempted, unsuccessfully due to police intervention, to "lay the cornerstone of the Third Temple" on the Temple Mount, an event which stirred high emotions in Umm al-Fahm and elsewhere and occasioned the editorial in *Sawt al-Haqq* cited above. Sheikh Ra'id is quoted to have said, on that occasion:

> The Aqsa Mosque is the heart which gives us life and unity and it stands above all political decisions which may be taken day in, day out....The Temple cornerstone affair is but one expression of the larger scheme which has preceded it. We read in the *Protocols of the Elders of Zion* that the Third Temple must be built on the ruins of the Aqsa Mosque. The schemes are many fold: first, tourists were allowed to enter the Mosque, the Jews were permitted to pray there, and then excavations were undertaken around it and tunnels were dug underneath it in order to facilitate the blowing up of the Mosque.[44] And let us not forget the arson of the Mosque.[45] Therefore, we must transcend proposals and resolutions and go over to acts and deeds.[46]

Sawt al-Haqq also addresses itself to current affairs and takes a position whenever the case of the Arabs or the Muslims seems compromised. Apart from the perennial articles about the martyrs of the intifada since the Palestinian uprising broke out in 1987, anniversaries such as the arson of the Aqsa mosque, or the outbreak of wars against Israel, and the special sympathetic emphasis on the activities of the Hamas in the territories, the journal also abounds with other issues which reveal the concerns of its editors and writers. A case in point has been the repeated appeal to Moscow to repeal open Jewish immigration to Israel[47] ("to our country" in Islamic parlance). The Muslim movement demanded that it be allowed, "just like the Jews," to publish their protests in the Soviet press. Their rationale was that "the liberation of Palestine is a national, patriotic and Islamic duty," and the Soviets could not be expected to fight for the Islamic cause against Israel.[48]

Other Muslim fundamentalist journals which appear outside Israel are also often cited by *Sawt al-Haqq*. One of them, *Filastin-al-Muslima*, which is printed in Britain, was quoted in November 1989, during the height of the intifada, to signify that the struggle of the Muslim movement, in Israel, in the territories, as well as outside of them, was not only over what it perceives as the occupied territories, but indeed over Palestine as a whole:

I was scanning through the books when the tears of Haifa and the sighs of Ramla and the Triangle[49] were crying to me. The map of Palestine has been telling me that Haifa and Jaffa take precedence over Jenin and Nablus....Your sighs are but the beloved melody of the oranges of Haifa and Jaffa and of the walls of Acre....The map of Palestine is weeping over its sons who were dispossessed forty years ago....Their story is horrible....We shall not forget Hebron, Jaffa and the Galilee. Our road is long but the [Israeli] prisons shall not obstruct it. O, the Prophet of Allah! We shall recuperate the Aqsa Mosque and Haifa.[50]

However, those same irredentist claims are not only insinuated by proxy, they are also directly and unequivocally advanced in other articles of the journal:

I shall imprint on the olive trees the story of the human predatory beasts who devour human flesh...of the criminals and arch-murderers who have massacred my people and persecuted it to the extreme confines of the Arab west. I shall write a poem of anger and hatred to this occupier, and a poem of love to every inch of the land of Jerusalem, Haifa, Jenin, Jericho, the Triangle....I shall not rest as long as the descendants of the Prophet lie in jail.[51]

Sawt al-Haqq also publishes letters, poems and other contributions from Muslim fundamentalists in the territories who profess the same values of retrieving all Palestine and eliminating Israel,[52] dehumanizing Israel and delegitimizing it by accusing it of systematically annihilating the Palestinians and desecrating Muslim holy shrines, and calling upon Muslim youth to die as martyrs. They justify all attempts of terrorism against Israel and condemn Israel when it tries the "innocent" culprits,[53] and indulge in outright encouragement and incitement of the participants in the intifada to pursue their "holy fight of rocks, because rocks are the weapon of Allah....The Prophet also had used rocks in his combat against the unbelievers in Badr and that weapon proved lethal...which shows that rocks are a holy weapon."[54] In one of its issues, *Sawt al-Haqq* urged Muslims to desist from emigration, because Palestine is the "land of the Isra' and Mi'raj"[55] and "the land of Jerusalem, Jaffa, Nablus, the Galilee, the

Negev, is the land of Allah."[56] A tenth grader from the state-sponsored and financed Middle School of Umm al-Fahm wrote a poem for the journal in which he said, inter alia, "Carry your weapon, for the days are coming when Islam will win and the rascals will be defeated."[57]

The Muslim movement's press based in Umm al-Fahm does not only seek its propagation on the merit of its editorial policy, but explicitly urges the "diffusion of the Islamic press with pride" and announces assemblies and public gatherings in order to "explain the nature of the Islamic press." For, as the editors view it: "Our publications are written expressions of our preaching, while the tangible manifestations of our preaching can be found in our activities and endeavors such as work camps, clinics, colleges, Islamic associations, soccer teams, etc." In other words, since Islam impregnates all aspects of life, the Islamic press, specifically *Al-Sirat* and *Sawt al-Haqq wal-Huriyya*, are "the authentic voice of the Islamic movement in the Holy Land," and anyone who subscribes to that press thereby "strengthens the march forward of the movement."[58] Thus, the Islamic movement and its press are at the disposal of all Islamic movements. Following the elections in Jordan in late 1989, where the Muslim fundamentalists took over more than a third of the seats in the new parliament, *Sawt al-Haqq* published a poem in honor of that sister-movement and its venerated head, Sheikh Yussuf al-'Azm:

When will magnificence return to our beloved East and when will glory return to our Nation?
When the pointed swords shall return,
Then the arrogant enemy will be routed and oppressed, then their bastion will collapse on the heads of its builders,[59]
Then the ancestors[60] will return to restore its ruins....
O Brothers[61] in our Jordan,[62] you are harbingers of good tidings....
O 'Azm! Men of honor always carry out their word! Here is the Galilee, here is the Port-city[63] and here is Jerusalem,
the Pearl of the East and the Universe which houses the Great Structure.[64]
O Yussuf, we are sending you our blessings, we the prisoners,
This is a word of oath for the land of Galilee.[65]

Subsequent issues of the journal called upon the Muslim Brothers in Jordan to "continue to march forward until the entire land falls into Muslim hands."[66] On their part, they undertook to expel the Israelis from western Palestine by urging them to "go away from my homeland, you treacherous murderer and usurper."[67] They went as far as demeaning the Jews by claiming that they are impure and therefore when they, the "enemies of Allah," step on carpets inside mosques they defile the place; but there is a built-in remedy in that inextricable situation: "the purest part of the Jews are their shoes[68] because they are in permanent contact with our pure land."[69] Still fearing the consequences of their open-enough incitement to revolt against Israel within its boundaries, they refrain from more explicit terms when they declare:

> We aim at all the Muslim people and therefore we want the banner of Allah to be rehoisted anew over the lands that used to be part of the Islamic realm at any time in history[70] and where the voice of the Muazzin used to be heard.[71] We want this call to get to all inhabitants of the world, everyone of these stages[72] has its significance and ramifications, but we are refraining at this point from going into more details and revealing more.[73]

Notes

*   This chapter is part of a study entitled "Islamic Fundamentalism in Israel," to appear as a book (London: Brassey's, forthcoming).

1.   Thomas Mayer, "Muslim Youth in Israel," *The New East* (Hebrew) Vol. XXXIII (1989): 10-11.

2.   For these statistics and their significance, see R. Paz, "The Islamic Movement in Israel following the Mayoral Elections," *Data and Analysis* (Dayan Center, Tel Aviv University, May 1989).

3.   The details of Sheikh Ra'id's role in the Islamic movement are drawn from interviews with members of the movement and from Gideon Samet's wide-ranging article on the subject, *Haaretz* (20 October 1989), p. 35.

4. Some of the material used in this passage and the next is based on Atallah Mansur's article in *Haaretz* (6 March 1989), which was confirmed and expanded in interviews with local Muslim activists.

5. *Ibid.*

6. A contemporary Muslim fundamentalist periodical in Norway is called *Al-Sabil* (the Path).

7. The Jalalayn authoritative commentary of the Qur'an is quite explicit: Those who earn Allah's anger are the Jews and those who go astray are the Christians, and therefore they are not part of those favored by Allah to "follow the Straight Path."

8. See Th. Mayer, "The Muslim Youth in Israel" (Hebrew), in A. Layish, ed., *The New East,* Vol. XXXII, No. 125-8 (1989): 18.

9. The Palestinian uprising in the West Bank and Gaza which began on December 8, 1987 and showed no sign of receding by the summer of 1990.

10. Mayer, *op. cit.*, p. 19.

11. R. Paz, "The Islamic Movement in Israel, following the Elections to the Local Councils (February 1989)," (Dayan Center for Middle Eastern Studies, Tel Aviv University, May 1989), p. 16.

12. For the summary and interpretation of that article, see Paz, *op. cit.*, pp. 18-19.

13. *Ibid.*, p. 19.

14. *Al-Sirat* monthly, November 1988.

15. The first is the Second Caliph of the Prophet who is credited with the conquest of Palestine and Jerusalem and the establishment of the first foundations of the Muslim empire; the second is the great general of the early Islamic conquests; and the third is Saladin, the renowned Kurdish-Muslim fighter and statesman who recovered Palestine, including Jerusalem, from the Crusaders.

16. *Al-Sirat* monthly, December 1988.

17. See, for example, *Al-Sirat* monthly of July 1989 and November 1989.

18. The Holocaust Memorial in Jerusalem.

19. *Al-Sirat* weekly, 24 March 1989.

20. The hill area east of the coastal plain of Israel where much of the Arab population of Israel is concentrated.

21. *Al-Sirat* weekly, 24 March 1989.

22. *Al-Sirat* weekly, 29 April 1989; see also 9 June 1989.

23. *Al-Sirat* weekly, 12 May 1989.

24. *Al-Sirat* weekly, 26 May 1989.

25. Oral tradition imparted to the Prophet Muhammad.

26. *Al-Sirat* weekly, 30 June 1989.

27. *Al-Sirat* weekly, 4 August 1989.

28. *Al-Sirat* weekly, 21 July 1989.

29. *Al-Sirat* weekly, 4 August 1989.

30. A less serious case of incitement against Jews in Stockholm, Sweden, by Radio Islam under the direction of Sheikh Ahmed Rami, occasioned a prosecution by the state attorney, which ended in the indictment of the Sheikh and the closing down of his station. See Chapter 9.

31. The area of the holy shrines of Mecca and Medina in Saudi Arabia.

32. *Al-Sirat* weekly, 18 August 1989.

33. *Al-Sirat* weekly, 1 September 1989.

34. *Ibid.*

35. *Ibid.*

36. E.g., a 15-month-old child who throws a rock at an Israeli soldier who responds with a point-blank shot at the child's head and then reports that "an extremist Palestinian guilty of incitement has been liquidated," *Al-Sirat* weekly, 1 September 1989.

37. *Al-Sirat* weekly, 8 September 1989.

38. E.g., *Al-Sirat* weekly, 22 September 1989.

39. *Ibid.*

40. See, e.g., *Al-Sirat* weekly, 29 September 1989 and 6 October 1989.

41. *Al-Sirat* weekly, 6 October 1989.

42. *Sawt al-Haqq wal-Huriyya* (henceforth, *SHWH*), 13 October 1989 and 20 October 1989.

43. *SHWH*, 27 October 1989.

44. For years, the Israeli authorities have been indeed excavating around the Temple Mount for archeological purposes, and digging a long tunnel along the Western Wall in order to uncover the long-buried strata of the original wall surrounding the Jewish Temple. That work was largely completed by early 1990 and the premises are open to tourists and visitors. No substantial damage is known to have occurred to the Muslim holy sites as a result.

45. In August 1969, an Australian tourist, Michael Rohan, attempted to burn down the Mosque. Israeli authorities put out the fire, arrested the culprit and indicted him, but most Muslims around the world, including those of Israel, have been accusing Israeli authorities ever since of collusion with that criminal tourist in kindling the flames of arson. Umm al-Fahm's locally published journals, newspapers and leaflets have since repeated that accusation on the anniversary of the arson.

46. *SHWH*, 27 October 1989.

47. *Ibid.* As a matter of fact, the article urged the Soviet Union to issue a "White Paper" to stop Jewish immigration into Israel, making a clear allusion to the British White Paper issued to the same effect in the 1930s under Arab pressure, the consequence of which was that Jewish refugees from Nazi persecution were not allowed into Palestine and most of them were returned to Europe and annihilated during the Holocaust.

48. *Ibid.*

49. All areas of Israel since its foundation in 1948.
50. *Filastin al-Muslima* (Muslim Palestine), Britain, cited by *SHWH*, 3 November 1989.

51. *SHWH*, 3 November 1989.

52. A contributor from Jenin wrote: O fighter for the Cause of Allah (Mujahid), rise, the walls of Acre are urging you....You cannot be considered dead, you are a war hero....*Heresy* is ripe for harvest. So, take up the scythe and saturate the thirst of the Believers for vengeance, for the fire is burning in the hearts of the widows. The meager sheep has worn the cloak of a lion; they have massacred pregnant women. *SHWH*, 3 November 1981.

53. *SHWH*, 10 November 1989.

54. *SHWH*, 17 November 1989.

55. These two terms refer to the Muslim belief in the nighttime journey of the Prophet from Mecca to Jerusalem and his ascension to Heaven, respectively.

56. In Hamas statements, all the land of Palestine is indeed referred to as a "waqf," a holy endowment. See *SHWH*, 17 November 1989.

57. *SHWH*, 24 November 1989.

58. *SHWH*, 1 December 1989.

59. An image alluding to the "Crusader Bastion" which had been destroyed by the Muslim Saladin in the twelfth century.

60. This refers to the first generation of Palestinian refugees who were displaced in 1948 after the foundation of Israel and the war which ensued.

61. "Brothers" is a double-pun: brothers as Arabs and Muslims and "Muslim Brothers."

62. "Our Jordan" can imply the context of the whole of historical Palestine, including Jordan, in which the idea of an Islamic state would be implemented.

63. Obvious reference to Jaffa, which was the main harbor on the Palestinian coast during most of the history of the land.

64. The Aqsa Mosque is meant in that appellation.

65. Umm al-Fahm is located in the lower reaches of the Galilee. See *SHWH*, 1 December 1989.

66. *SHWH*, 22 December 1989.

67. *SHWH*, 8 December 1989.

68. In Arab tradition, shoes are considered mean and dirty, and therefore when one has to refer to them as a necessity, one adds "far from you," as a way of exonerating oneself from that terrible act of discourtesy. Here, the shoes are the best part of the Jews, how much more impure are their bodies!

69. *SHWH*, 8 December 1989.

70. *Dar-al-Islam*, the lands that had come, at one time or another, under Islamic rule, including Israel, Spain and Portugal, and Southern France, and are to be recovered ultimately and brought back under Islamic rule.

71. The *muazzin* calls the believers for prayer from the top of the minarets of all mosques. The call for prayer came to symbolize the extent of Islamic presence across areas occupied by Islam.

72. The "strategy of stages" developed by the PLO in the 1970s, meaning that Palestine could be recovered piecemeal instead of at one stroke, has been embraced by the Islamic movement too, in an "Islamic" version. Indeed, in another of its publications (*SHWH*, 12 January 1990), the Islamic movement refers to the "state of total liberation" as the ultimate goal of the Muslims.

73. *SHWH*, 29 December 1989.

121

Chapter 7

THE CHARTER OF ALLAH: THE PLATFORM OF THE ISLAMIC RESISTANCE MOVEMENT (HAMAS)*

Author's Introduction

Historical Background

The contemporary rise of Islamic fundamentalism among the Palestinian Arabs is not without antecedents. In the 1920s, Izz a-Din al-Qassam, a Syrian Muslim who settled in Haifa, became the Imam of the Istiqlal Mosque there, and undertook extensive religious, political and educational activities in northern Palestine, which soon lent prominence to his leadership. He began his career as a preacher and organizer and in the early 1930s formed a militant group, *al-kaff al-Aswad* (The Black Hand) as an instrument of struggle against British imperialism and Jewish Zionism in the land. In 1935, he called openly for *jihad* against both, but he and his followers were intercepted by the British authorities and crushed. Qassam himself died in the battle which ensued.[1]

The next wave of fundamentalism among Palestinian Muslims was prompted by the society of the Muslim Brothers which was founded in Egypt in the late 1920s and spread from there to other core areas of the Middle East. During the Palestinian Revolt of 1936-39, Abd-al-Rahman al-Banna, brother of Hassan al-Banna, the founder and first leader of the Muslim Brothers, visited Jerusalem, met with the Mufti and helped channel Brothers' funds and propaganda to the benefit of the Revolt. From these modest beginnings there developed, after World War II, a formidable network of the Brothers' presence in Palestine. The first Muslim Brothers group in Palestine was established in 1946, followed later that year by more chapters in Jaffa, Lydda, Haifa, Nablus and Tulkarem.[2] In all, 25 branches of the Brothers were established in western Palestine, whose active membership was estimated at close to 20,000.[3]

The activism of the Brothers was two-pronged, exactly like its Qassamite antecedent: *jihad* against both British occupation and Zionist aspirations. To this end, the Brothers engaged in para-military training of its adherents, but apparently due to their sporadic nature, under the open eyes of the British authorities, these efforts did not bear much fruit. Local members of the Brothers did partici-pate in the war against fledgling Israel in 1948, alongside larger contingents dispatched from Egypt and to some extent from Syria and Transjordan as well.[4]

The 1948 War between the Arabs and Israel, and the consequent Armistice Agreements between the parties signed in 1949, split the Palestinian Arab population into an Israeli-ruled minority and a Jordanian and Egyptian-governed majority, in the West Bank and the Gaza Strip, respectively. Under Israel, the Arab community found itself exhausted, disoriented, impoverished and humiliated; its Mus-lim activity fell into disarray and therefore the role of the Muslim Brothers lost its steam and went into abeyance. One insignificant exception was the tiny "Shabab Muhammad" (Muhammad's Youth) organization which sprang up in the Galilee in the mid-1960s. The Palestinians of the West Bank and Gaza, however, emboldened by the active participation of the Brothers in 1948, and shocked by the disaster (*nakbah*) of the loss of parts of Palestine to the Jews, swelled the ranks of the Muslim Brothers in those two territories after 1949.

In the West Bank, there was widespread distribution of the literature of the movement and rather ramified social and cultural activities, especially among the youth, such as scouting and sports organizations. Moreover, while all other political parties were banned most of the time by the Hashemite Crown, the Brothers were permit-ted to deploy a network of branches and to conduct their affairs openly. This did not mean that the Brothers were reticent to criticize the society amidst which they operated: they indeed occasionally criticized Jordan's close links to the West, the public consumption of alcohol, and the loose interpretations of the Muslim Holy Law (Shari'a).[5] The dual position of the Brothers as an accepted legal organization, on the one hand, and as a critique of society, on the other, produced an ambivalent stance of the organization towards the Crown: at times, when criticism and friction with the authorities became too evident, the regime tightened the controls over the Brothers and even arrested some of its leaders; at other times, they won the favor of the king due to their consistent anti-nationalistic, anti-communist, anti-Baathist and anti-Nasserite stands which served the interests of the Hashemite court.

The Muslim Brothers were not alone in the West Bank waving the flag of fundamentalist Islam. Another faction, the Islamic Liberation Party (Hizb a-Tahrir al-Islami), contended with similar views and attracted similar constituencies. Rivalry between the two movements ensued, which may have damaged their common cause, especially at a period when pan-Arabism, at its height under Nasser, was far more attractive to the masses than Islamic ideologies. In any case, the Muslim fundamentalist appeal, although well organized around a committed hard core of fundamentalist Muslims, remained marginal in Jordan's politics, as in the rest of the Arab world, until the waning of Nasserism and the Arab defeat of 1967. These Muslim elements did not manifest themselves in the struggle against Israel and did not participate in violence across its borders.[6]

In the Gaza Strip, on the other hand, the Muslim Brothers were far more active and militant, both domestically and externally as regards Israel. In the pre-revolution years (1949-52), the Brothers were banned in the Strip as they were in Egypt, and their activities were conducted underground. During the first two years of the revolution (1952-54), when the Brothers seemed to close ranks with the authorities, its membership increased as did the level of its activities, but they soon went underground again when their attempt on Nasser's life was revealed in Cairo and the movement was banned throughout Egypt. But by then, the Brothers had become the largest political movement in the Strip. The Brothers advocated armed resistance against Israel during the brief occupation of the Strip by the Israelis in 1956/57. Members of these armed *fedayeen* groups, which had been forming since 1954, later joined the Fatah and became PLO leaders.[7] The lull between Israel and Egypt in the period of 1956-1967 also signalled the significant weakening of the Brothers in the Strip, while Arab nationalist groups were in ascendance there.

Muslim Fundamentalists under Israeli Occupation

The occupation by Israel of the West Bank and the Gaza Strip during the 1967 War introduced new factors into the Islamic movement in western Palestine:

a) The swift removal of boundaries between Israel and the newly-occupied territories created a new self-awareness among the Arabs of those territories and the Arabs of Israel, an awareness which helped cement close and growing links between those hitherto separate components of the Palestinian people.

b) The struggle of the Muslim fundamentalists could now become focused on the Israeli enemy and on resistance to the occupation, a much more concrete and unifying theme for Muslims than the previous struggle against the Arab-Muslim governments which had ruled them.

c) Paradoxically, the Muslim movements could thrive under Israeli rule, which permitted their open activities as long as they did not contravene the law, much more than under the Arab governments which had ruled in the West Bank and Gaza.

d) Israel, which is viewed by Muslim fundamentalists as an extension of the West, threatened by its very presence and predomination to encroach upon the traditional value systems of the administered territories; only a vigorous response-by-negation by the fundamentalists could ward off what they regarded as an ideological onslaught of Israel designed to subvert Islam from within.

e) Israel's incursion into all fabrics of social, political and economic life in the territories finally dealt a deadly blow to the vestiges of the rule of the *a'yan* (notables) who had predominated in Palestinian politics after World War I.[8] Those notables, who struggled under the British Mandate both to maintain their status as guardians of the holy places in Palestine and to prevent the establishment of a Jewish National Home there, had used the symbols of Jerusalem and the Holy Land to counter those perceived threats. With the notables gone as predominant figures in Palestinian politics, and in view of the avowedly secular leadership offered by the PLO, Palestinians concerned about political Islam turned to fundamentalist movements.

To be sure, these elements of Islam, which are used as a part of the national struggle of the Palestinians, are not monopolized by "fundamentalist" groups. The mainstream of Palestinian nationalism itself has used Islam, as Johnson has shown,[9] to characterize enemies, to imply modes of action against them, and to define the nature of the Palestinian community and its struggle, thus linking key religious and secular concepts. *Jihad*, for example, links with "revolution," that is, a violent political struggle; the commitment to

126

fight against imperialism being a contemporary manifestation of the historical presence of the West in the Muslim Middle East which goes back to the times of the Crusades. When the PLO calls its casualties *shuhada* (martyrs) and its guerrillas *fidaiin*, it is clear that they imply the redemption inherent in dying for one's homeland, in the Muslim sense of the concept, since *fida'i* equals a *mujahid* (fighter for the cause of *jihad*, the Holy War)."[10] Similarly, the struggle against the Jews or Zionists, two terms often used interchangeably, harks back to the old Jewish-Muslim enmity of the times of the Prophet. Thus, when Chairman Arafat made the *haj* (pilgrimage) to Mecca in 1978, he declared the liberation of Palestine a commandment of Allah that no Muslim was excepted from. That liberation was to be a *jihad* to recover all Palestine, including Jerusalem. Furthermore, even the seemingly secular document of the Palestinian Covenant, adopted in 1964 and amended in 1968, is interspersed with concepts that can be seen as Islamic: sacrifice, struggle, armed struggle; Article 16 refers to the issue of Palestine as a Holy Land with religious sites. At the Algiers Conference where the Palestinians declared their independence (on 15 November 1988), Jerusalem is referred to as the capital city, whereas it had been regarded before as merely the seat and permanent headquarters of the PLO.

That the PLO has been manipulating Islamic symbols should come as no surprise, for Islam is too important a part of the Palestinian culture and people to ignore. However, while the PLO handles Islam like other Muslim regimes by controlling it, the fundamentalists in the territories are much more passionate and much less patient than the political leaders of their national movement seem to be. They want everything here and now; they lend primacy to Islam over nationalistic and other considerations; and they are more prepared than others to risk their necks in the fulfillment of those lofty goals.

Since the Israeli takeover of the territories in 1967 and up until the end of the 1970s, the Islamic fundamentalist activity there was largely suspended,[11] probably due to the Muslim Brothers' reluctance to challenge the nationalist movement of the Palestinians under the PLO's aegis, which was at the height of its popularity in those years. However, the success of the Iranian Revolution (1979), followed by the assassination of President Sadat (1981), who had been repudiated as a traitor to Islam, and the mounting Islamic resistance against Israel in the wake of the Lebanese War (1982-83), have all lent impetus to Islam as a political force pregnant with change and victory. The dormant Islamic movement in the territories elected to ride the crest of these events and to identify with them, and this helped pull it out of its torpor and build it into an unstated alternative force to the failing conventional Palestinian nationalism.

In the 1980s, the Islamic bloc emerged as a powerful constituency in the local politics of the territories, boosted by the three Islamic colleges of Jerusalem, Gaza and Hebron, established in 1978. The Muslim Brothers remains the largest and most influential faction, seconded by the smaller Liberation Party. These elements are particularly visible in the universities of the territories, but their adherents are spread throughout the area. They consist of large groups of quietists who see Israeli occupation as a punishment for the deviation of Muslims from the path of Allah, and therefore they seek the solution for the plight of the Palestinians in the return to the way of God; and small but growing bands of hardcore militants have embraced the Iranian model of revolution where a committed but activist group had succeeded in toppling a strong but unpopular government backed by the U.S.[12]

The Muslim Brothers has embraced a wide-ranging political, cultural and social program which, in the absence of a Palestinian national authority in the territories, purports to outline patterns of conduct to counter the occupying power, and to gradually create an anti-state which would ultimately replace the withdrawing government of the Israelis. In the late 1980s and 1990s, this movement was represented by the Hamas, *Harakat Muqawama Islamiyya* (the Movement of Islamic Resistance), the acronym also signifying "devotion," "enthusiasm," and "zeal" in the path of Allah. Judging from its active participation in the intifada, its series of public pronouncements which are calculated to compete with the PLO, and its political platform released in late 1988, this fundamentalist movement seems to articulate a growing sentiment among the Palestinians that Islam is the panacea for all the ills of Palestine.

The Hamas Charter

To gain an insight into this movement's program, let us first summarize its publicized platform:

a) The Hamas is committed to Holy War for Palestine against the Jews, until the victory of Allah is implemented.

b) The land must be cleansed from the impurity and viciousness of the tyrannical occupiers.

c) Under the wings of Islam, coexistence is possible with members of other faiths. When Islam does not prevail then bigotry, hatred, controversy, corruption and oppression prevail.

d) The Muslims are under obligation, by order of their Prophet, to fight Jews and kill them wherever they can find them.

e) The Hamas strives to establish an entity where Allah is the ultimate goal, the Qur'an its constitution, *jihad* its means, death for the cause of Allah its sublimest aspiration.

f) The land of Palestine is a holy Islamic endowment (*waqf*) until the end of days. Thus, no one can negotiate it away.

g) It is the personal religious duty (*fard 'ayn*) of each individual Muslim to carry out this *jihad* in order to bring redemption to the land.

h) The Hamas is opposed to all international conferences and negotiations and to any peaceful settlements. For sovereignty over the land is a religious act and negotiating over it means yielding some of it to the rule of the unbelievers.

i) The Jews have taken over the world media and financial centers. By fomenting revolutions, wars, and such movements as the Freemasons, communism, capitalism, Zionism, Rotary, Lions, B'nai B'rith, etc., they are subverting human society as a whole in order to bring about its destruction, propagate their own viciousness and corruption, and take over the world via such of their pet institutions as the League of Nations, the U.N. and the Security Council. Their schemes are detailed in the *Protocols of the Elders of Zion.*

j) The Hamas opposed the PLO secular state in Palestine because it would be anti-Islamic in essence. But if the PLO adopts Islam as its path, then all members of the movement will become soldiers of liberation and will "produce the fire that will smite the enemy."

The 36-article Charter of Hamas, although it has interesting parallels with the 1968 PLO Charter in terms of the comprehensiveness, totality and virulence of its negation of Israel, bears nevertheless some very distinct characteristics:

First, while the PLO document was deliberated, debated, argued, amended, and voted upon before it was adopted by the Palestinian

National Council, the Hamas document was apparently concocted by some of its heads and then announced to the public.

Second, although both documents are called "Charter" (*mithaq*), it is evident that the PLO's is considered as a man-given constitutional-political document, which provides for the instrument of its amendment (Article 33). The Hamas document, by contrast, creates the impression of reflecting universal, eternal and Allah-given truths that are not liable to alterations, debates and questions. This means that while the former is amendable, when the political will exists, the latter is unalterable and immutable once it was put down on paper and publicized.

Third, the PLO Charter avoids direct antisemitic attacks on Jews as such and purports to struggle against Zionism only, while the Hamas document repeats accusations taken directly from the *Protocols of the Elders of Zion* and other notorious antisemitic writings.

Fourth, while the PLO Charter uses political language, intertwined with Arab-Islamic rhetoric, the Hamas Charter is wholly based on, and consistently draws from, the language of Islam.[13] Not only Islamic symbols are invoked, but all the political ramifications of the platform derive from Islam and are couched in Islamic terms. Often, the document's articles are backed by Qur'anic verses, which lend to it its immutable quality.

Fifth, the Hamas regards the entire Islamic world as its constituency and seeks support therefrom. Its message is pan-Islamic and extra-national; the PLO relies more on Arab nationalism and views the Arab states as its backers and partners.

Sixth, the PLO plan is not only substantive but also organizational and institutional; it sets forth the steps to be followed with a view of annihilating Zionism and of substituting for it a new Palestinian political entity. Hamas' vision is one of an Islamic state over the entire land of Palestine, as part of the revived Islamic *umma*, but it does not envisage the substantive and institutional means through which this would be achieved.

Seventh, the PLO program purported to resolve the status of Jews in the land of Palestine by reducing their numbers and granting political rights to the remaining minority. The Hamas Charter explicitly states that the non-Muslims of the revealed religions would be treated according to the *dhimmi* status.

Eighth, while the PLO regards itself as an independent *wataniyya* (local patriotism), in the framework of Arab *qawmiyya* (ethnocultural Arab nationalism), the Hamas declares its affiliation with the Muslim Brothers of Egypt from whose ideology they draw their message and on whose masters they rely for guidance.

Ninth, at a time when the PLO has been, at least on the surface, attempting to adopt diplomatic means and political measures in its endeavor to gain international recognition, the Hamas seems to be oblivious of the world community. For the Islamic movement, any international wheeling and dealing amounts to a "loss of time" and any intercession of the foreign powers in the Arab-Israeli conflict is tantamount to imperialism's "collusion" with Zionism.

Tenth, the PLO Charter is totally committed to a political and military program in order to attain Palestinian self-determination and nationhood from the powers-that-be, while the Hamas platform commits itself to a socio-cultural and religious-moral mode of action in order to raise Islamic consciousness and to conquer Muslim societies from within before it conquers the rest.

The importance of the Hamas lies not only in its rather strident and uncompromising message, but even more so in its rising profile and popularity among the Palestinians in the territories and even in Israel, where the Islamic movement, an avowed cousin of the Hamas, has made impressive strides forward during the decade of the 1980s, culminating in the successes of the movement's leaders in the Israeli municipal elections in early 1989. It stands to reason that the less effective the PLO proves to be in attaining its political goals, the more the Islamic movement, including the Hamas, will find itself strengthened. Already some 40 percent of the Palestinian population of the Gaza Strip are said to follow the movement, and a somewhat lower percentage of sympathizers is estimated for the West Bank.[14] In any case, during the intifada, the Hamas has been able, on several occasions, to challenge the monopoly of the PLO, especially of the dominant Fatah group therein. Another prospect for the growth of the Hamas may derive from the dynamics of the intifada, on the one hand, and the facade of moderation of the PLO, on the other. For, as the sacrifices and the losses of the Palestinians in the territories yield no results, many of them will turn, in despair, to the good, old and familiar Islam as a source of sustenance and comfort. The PLO, which is perceived as diluting its message and losing its zeal, all in vain, may be sidestepped by the totalitarian and absolutist appeal of the Hamas. Loud, clear and sharp messages have always attracted the disaffected more than hesitant, blurred and soft half–measures.

* * *

THE CHARTER OF THE HAMAS[15]

In the Name of Allah, the Merciful, the Compassionate:
You are the best community that has been raised up for mankind.
Ye enjoin right conduct and forbid indecency; and ye believe in
Allah. And if the People of the Scripture[16] had believed, it had been
better for them. Some of them are believers; but most of them are
evil-doers.

They will not harm you save a trifling hurt, and if they fight
against you they will turn and flee. And afterward they will not be
helped.

"Ignominy shall be their portion wheresoever they are found
save [where they grasp] a rope from Allah and a rope from man.[17]
They have incurred anger from their Lord, and wretchedness is laid
upon them. That is because they used to disbelieve the revelations of
Allah, and slew the Prophets wrongfully. That is because they were
rebellious and used to transgress." *Surat Al-Imran (III), verses 109-
111.*[18]

"Israel will rise and will remain erect until Islam eliminates it as
it had eliminated its predecessors."
The Imam and Martyr Hassan al-Banna[19]
May Allah Pity his Soul

"The Islamic World is burning. It is incumbent upon each one of
us to pour some water, little as it may be, with a view of extinguishing
as much of the fire as he can, without awaiting action by the others."
Sheikh Amjad Al-zahawi
May Allah Pity his soul

In the name of Allah, the Merciful, the Compassionate:

Introduction

Grace to Allah, whose help we seek, whose forgiveness we
beseech, whose guidance we implore and on whom we rely. We pray
and bid peace upon the Messenger of Allah, his family, his compan-

ions, his followers and those who spread his message and followed his tradition; they will last as long as there exist Heaven and Earth.
O, people!

In the midst of misadventure, from the depth of suffering, from the believing hearts and purified arms; aware of our duty and in response to the decree of Allah, we direct our call,[20] we rally together and join each other. We educate in the path of Allah and we make our firm determination prevail so as to take its proper role in life, to overcome all difficulties and to cross all hurdles. Hence our permanent state of preparedness and our readiness to sacrifice our souls and dearest [possessions] in the path of Allah.

Thus, our nucleus has formed which chartered its way in the tempestuous ocean of creeds and hopes, desires and wishes, dangers and difficulties, setbacks and challenges, both internal and external.

When the thought matured, the seed grew and the plant took root in the land of reality, detached from temporary emotion and unwelcome haste, the Islamic Resistance Movement erupted in order to play its role in the path of its Lord. In so doing, it joined its hands with those of all *jihad*[21] fighters for the purpose of liberating Palestine. The souls of its *jihad* fighters will encounter those of all *jihad* fighters who have sacrificed their lives in the land of Palestine since it was conquered[22] by the Companion[23] of the Prophet, be Allah's prayer and peace upon him, and until this very day. This is the Charter of the Islamic Resistance (Hamas) which will reveal its face, unveil its identity, state its position, clarify its purpose, discuss its hopes, call for support to its cause and reinforcement, and for joining its ranks. For our struggle against the Jews is extremely wide-ranging and grave, so much so that it will need all the loyal efforts we can wield, to be followed by further steps and reinforced by successive battalions from the multifarious Arab and Islamic world, until the enemies are defeated and Allah's victory prevails. Thus we shall perceive them approaching on the horizon, and this will be known before long.

"Allah has decreed: Lo! I very shall conquer, I and my messenger, lo! Allah is strong, almighty." *Sura 58 (Al-Mujadilah), verse 21.*[24]

*   *   *

"Say: This is my way: I call on Allah with sure knowledge, I and whosoever follows me. Glory be to Allah! and I am not of the idolaters." *Sura 12 (Yussuf), verse 17 (108 in Pickthall).*

Part I — Knowing The Movement

The Ideological Aspects

Article One

The Islamic Resistance Movement draws its guidelines from Islam; derives from it its thinking, interpretations and views about existence, life and humanity; refers back to it for its conduct; and is inspired by it in whatever step it takes.

The Link between Hamas and the Association of Muslim Brothers

Article Two

The Islamic Resistance Movement is one of the wings of the Muslim Brothers in Palestine. The Muslim Brothers is a world organization, the largest Islamic movement in the modern era. It is characterized by a profound understanding, by precise notions and by a complete comprehensiveness of all concepts of Islam in all domains of life: views and beliefs, politics and economics, education and society, jurisprudence and rule, indoctrination and teaching, the arts and publications, the hidden and the evident, and all the other domains of life.

Structure and Essence

Article Three

The basic structure of the Islamic Resistance Movement consists of Muslims who are devoted to Allah and worship Him verily [as it is written]: "I have created Man and Devil for the purpose of their worship" [of Allah]. Those Muslims are cognizant of their duty towards themselves, their families and country, and they have been relying on Allah for all that. They have raised the banner of *jihad* in the face of the oppressors in order to extricate the country and the people from the [oppressors'] desecration, filth and evil.

"Nay, but we hurl the true against the false; and it does break its head and lo! it vanishes." *Sura 21 (the Prophets), verse 18.*

Article Four

The Movement welcomes all Muslims who share its beliefs and thinking, commit themselves to its course of action, keep its secrets and aspire to join its ranks in order to carry out their duty. Allah will reward them.

Dimensions of Time and Space of the Hamas

Article Five

As the movement adopts Islam as its way of life, its time dimension extends back as far as the birth of the Islamic message and of the Righteous Ancestor. Its ultimate goal is Islam, the Prophet its model, the Qur'an its constitution. Its special dimension extends wherever on earth there are Muslims, who adopt Islam as their way of life; thus, it penetrates to the deepest reaches of the land and to the highest spheres of heaven.

"Seest you not how Allah coins a similitude: a goodly saying, as a goodly tree, its root set firm, its branches reaching into heaven: Giving its fruit at every season by permission of its Lord? Allah coins the similitudes for mankind in order that they may reflect." *Sura 14 (Abraham), verses 24-25.*

Peculiarity and Independence

Article Six

The Islamic Resistance Movement is a distinct Palestinian Movement which owes its loyalty to Allah, derives from Islam its way of life and strives to raise the banner of Allah over every inch of Palestine. Only under the shadow of Islam could the members of all religions coexist in safety and security for their lives, properties and rights.[25] In the absence of Islam, conflict arises, oppression reigns, corruption is rampant and struggles and wars prevail. Allah had inspired the Muslim poet, Muhammad Iqbal,[26] when he said: When the Faith wanes, there is no security. There is no this-worldliness for those who have no faith. Those who wish to live their life without religion have made annihilation the equivalent of life.

The Universality of the Hamas

Article Seven

By virtue of the distribution of Muslims, who pursue the cause of the Hamas all over the globe, and strive for its victory, for the reinforcement of its positions and for the encouragement of its *jihad*, the movement is a universal one. It is apt to be that due to the clarity of its thinking, the nobility of its purpose and the loftiness of its objectives.

It is in this light that the movement has to be regarded, evaluated and acknowledged. Whoever denigrates its worth, or avoids supporting it, or is so blind as to dismiss its role, is challenging fate itself. Whoever closes his eyes from seeing the facts, whether intentionally or not, will wake up to find himself overtaken by events, and will find no excuses to justify his position. Priority is reserved to the early comers.

Oppressing those who are closest to you is more of an agony to the soul than the impact of an Indian sword.

"And unto thee have we revealed the Scripture with the truth, confirming whatever scripture was before it, and a watcher over it. So judge between them by that which Allah hath revealed, and follow not their desires away from the truth which has come unto thee. For each we have appointed a divine law and a traced-out way. Had Allah willed, He could have made you one community. But that He may try you by that which he has given you [He has made you as you are]. So vie with one another in good works. Unto Allah, you will all return. He will then inform you of that wherein you differ." *Sura V (the Table), verse 48.*

The Hamas is one of the links in the chain of *jihad* in the confrontation with the Zionist invasion. It links up with the setting out of the Martyr Izz a-din al-Qassam[27] and his brothers in the Muslim Brothers who fought the Holy War in 1936; it further relates to another link of the Palestinian *jihad* and the *jihad* and efforts of the Muslim Brothers during the 1948 War,[28] and to the *jihad* operations of the Muslim Brothers in 1968[29] and thereafter.

But even if the links have become distant from each other, and even if the obstacles erected by those who revolve in the Zionist orbit, aiming at obstructing the road before the *jihad* fighters, have rendered the pursuance of *jihad* impossible; nevertheless, the Hamas has been looking forward to implement Allah's promise whatever time it might take. The prophet, prayer and peace be upon him, said:

The time[30] will not come until Muslims will fight the Jews (and kill them); until the Jews hide behind rocks and trees, which will cry: O Muslim! there is a Jew hiding behind me, come on and kill him! This will not apply to the Gharqad,[31] which is a Jewish tree (cited by Bukhari and Muslim).[32]

The Slogan of the Hamas

Article Eight

Allah is its goal, the Prophet its model, the Qur'an its constitution, *jihad* its path, and death for the cause of Allah its most sublime belief.

Part II — Motives and Objectives

Article Nine

The Hamas finds itself at a period of time when Islam has waned away from the reality of life. For this reason, the checks and balances have been upset, concepts have become confused, and values have been transformed; evil has prevailed, oppression and obscurity have reigned; cowards have turned tigers, homelands have been usurped, people have been uprooted and are wandering all over the globe. The state of truth has disappeared and was replaced by the state of evil. Nothing has remained in its right place, for when Islam is removed from the scene, everything changes. These are the motives.

As to the objectives: discarding the evil, crushing it and defeating it, so that truth may prevail, homelands revert [to their owners], calls for prayer be heard from their mosques, announcing the reinstitution of the Muslim state. Thus, people and things will revert to their true place. Allah is the one whose hold we see.

"...And if Allah had not repelled some men by others the earth would have been corrupted. But Allah is the Lord of kindness to [His] creatures." *Sura II (the Cow), verse 251.*

Article Ten

The Islamic Resistance Movement, while breaking its own path, will do its utmost to constitute at the same time a support to the weak, a defense to all the oppressed. It will spare no effort to implement the truth and abolish evil, in speech and in fact, both here and in any other location where it can reach out and exert influence.

Part III — Strategies and Methods

The Strategy of Hamas: Palestine is an Islamic Waqf[33]

Article Eleven

The Islamic Resistance Movement believes that the land of Palestine has been an Islamic *waqf* throughout the generations and until the Day of Resurrection; no one can renounce it or part of it, or abandon it or part of it. No Arab country nor the aggregate of all Arab countries, and no Arab king or president, nor all of them in the aggregate, have that right, nor has any organization that right or the aggregate of all organizations, be they Palestinian or Arab, because Palestine is an Islamic *waqf* throughout all generations and to the Day of Resurrection. Who can presume to speak for all Islamic generations to the Day of Resurrection? This is the status [of the land] in Islamic Shari'a,[34] and it is similar to all lands conquered by Islam by force, and made thereby *waqf* lands upon their conquest, for all generations of Muslims until the Day of Resurrection. This [norm] has prevailed since the commanders of the Muslim armies completed the conquest of Syria and Iraq, and they asked the Caliph of Muslims, 'Umar Ibn al-Khattab,[35] for his view of the conquered land, whether it should be partitioned between the troops or left in the possession of its population, or otherwise. Following discussions and consultations between the Caliph of Islam, 'Umar Ibn al-Khattab, and the companions of the Messenger of Allah, be peace and prayer upon him, they decided that the land should remain in the hands of its owners to benefit from it and from its wealth; but the control[36] of the land and the land itself ought to be endowed as a *waqf* [in perpetuity] for all generations of Muslims until the Day of Resurrection. The ownership of the land by its owners is only one of usufruct, and this *waqf* will endure as long as heaven and earth last. Any demarche in violation of this law of Islam, with regard to Palestine, is baseless and reflects on its perpetrators.

"Lo! This is certain truth. Therefore, O Muhammad, praise the name of thy Lord, the Tremendous."*Sura LVI (the Event), verse 95.*[37]

The Hamas in Palestine: Its Views on Homeland and Nationalism[38]

Article Twelve

The Hamas regards nationalism (*wataniyya*) as part and parcel of the religious faith. Nothing is loftier or deeper in nationalism than waging *jihad* against the enemy and confronting him when he sets foot on the land of the Muslims. And this becomes an individual duty[39] binding on every Muslim man and woman; a woman must go out and fight the enemy even without her husband's authorization, and a slave without his masters' permission. This [principle] does not exist under any other regime, and it is a truth not to be questioned. While other nationalisms consist of material, human and territorial considerations, the nationality of the Hamas also carries, in addition to all those, the all-important divine factors which lend to it its spirit and life; so much so that it connects with the origin of the spirit and the source of life and raises in the skies of the homeland the banner of the Lord, thus inexorably connecting earth with heaven.

When Moses came and threw his baton, sorcery and sorcerers became futile.

"...The right direction is henceforth distinct from error. And he who rejects false deities and believes in Allah has grasped a firm handhold which will never break. Allah is Hearer, Knower." *Sura II (the Cow), verse 256.*[40]

Peaceful Solutions, [Peace] Initiatives and International Conferences

Article Thirteen

[Peace] initiatives, the so-called peaceful solutions, and the international conferences to resolve the Palestinian problem, are all contrary to the beliefs of the Islamic Resistance Movement. For renouncing any part of Palestine means renouncing part of the religion; the nationalism of the Islamic Resistance Movement is part of its faith, the movement educates its members to adhere to its principles and to raise the banner of Allah over their homeland as they fight their *jihad*: "Allah is the all-powerful, but most people are not aware."

From time to time a clamoring is voiced, to hold an international conference in search for a solution to the problem. Some accept the idea, others reject it, for one reason or another, demanding the implementation of this or that condition, as a prerequisite for agreeing to convene the conference or for participating in it. But the Islamic Resistance Movement, which is aware of the [prospective] parties to this conference, and of their past and present positions towards the problems of the Muslims, does not believe that those conferences are capable of responding to demands, or of restoring rights or doing justice to the oppressed. Those conferences are no more than a means to appoint the nonbelievers as arbitrators in the lands of Islam. Since when did the unbelievers do justice to the believers?

"And the Jews will not be pleased with thee, nor will the Christians, till thou follow their creed. 'Say: Lo! the guidance of Allah [himself] is the Guidance.' And if you should follow their desires after the knowledge which has come unto thee, then you would have from Allah no protecting friend nor helper." *Sura 2 (the Cow), verse 120.*

There is no solution to the Palestinian problem except by *jihad*. The initiatives, proposals and international conferences are but a waste of time,[41] an exercise in futility. The Palestinian people are too noble to have their future, their right and their destiny submitted to a vain game. As the *hadith* has it:

"The people of Syria are Allah's whip on this land; He takes revenge by their intermediary from whoever he wished among his worshipers. The hypocrites among them are forbidden from vanquishing the true believers, and they will die in anxiety and sorrow." (Told by Tabarani, who is traceable in ascending order of traditionaries to Muhammad, and by Ahmed, whose chain of transmission is incomplete. But it is bound to be a true *hadith*, for both storytellers are reliable. Allah knows best.)[42]

The Three Circles

Article Fourteen

The problem of the liberation of Palestine relates to three circles: the Palestinian, the Arab and the Islamic. Each one of these circles has a role to play in the struggle against Zionism and it has duties to fulfill. It would be an enormous mistake and an abysmal act of ignorance to disregard any one of these circles. For Palestine is an Islamic land where the First Qibla[43] and the third holiest site[44] are located. That is also the place whence the Prophet, be Allah's prayer and peace upon him, ascended to heavens.[45]

"Glorified be He who carried His servant by night from the Inviolable Place of Worship[46] to the Far Distant Place of Worship,[47] the neighborhood whereof we have blessed, that we might show him of our tokens! Lo! He, only He, is the Hearer, the Seer." *Sura XVII (al-Isra'), verse 1.*[48]

In consequence of this state of affairs, the liberation of that land is an individual duty binding on all Muslims everywhere.[49] This is the base on which all Muslims have to regard the problem; this has to be understood by all Muslims. When the problem is dealt with on this basis, where the full potential of the three circles is mobilized, then the current circumstances will change and the day of liberation will come closer.

"You are more awful as a fear in their bosoms than Allah. That is because they are a folk who understand not." *Sura LIX, (Al-Hashr, the Exile), verse 13.*

The Jihad for the Liberation of Palestine is an Individual Obligation[50]

Article Fifteen

When our enemies usurp some Islamic lands, *jihad* becomes a duty binding on all Muslims. In order to face the usurpation of Palestine by the Jews, we have no escape from raising the banner of *jihad*. This would require the propagation of Islamic consciousness among the masses on all local, Arab and Islamic levels. We must spread the spirit of *jihad* among the [Islamic] *umma*, clash with the enemies and join the ranks of the *jihad* fighters.

The *'ulama* as well as educators and teachers, publicity and media men as well as the masses of the educated, and especially the youth and the elders of the Islamic Movements, must participate in this raising of consciousness. There is no escape from introducing fundamental changes in educational curricula in order to cleanse them from all vestiges of the ideological invasion which has been brought about by orientalists and missionaries. That invasion had begun overtaking this area following the defeat of the Crusader armies by Salah a-Din el Ayyubi.[51] The Crusaders had understood that they had no way to vanquish the Muslims unless they prepared the grounds for that with an ideological invasion which would confuse the thinking of Muslims, revile their heritage, discredit their ideals, to be followed by a military invasion. That was to be in preparation for the imperialist invasion, as in fact [General] Allenby[52] acknowledged it upon his entry to Jerusalem: "Now, the Crusades are over." General Gouraud[53] stood on the tomb of Salah a-Din and declared: "We have returned, O Salah-a-Din!" Imperialism has been instrumental in boosting the ideological invasion and deepening its roots, and it is still pursuing this goal. All this had paved the way to the loss of Palestine. We must imprint on the minds of generations of Muslims that the Palestinian problem is a religious one, to be dealt with on this premise. It includes Islamic holy sites such as the Aqsa Mosque, which is inexorably linked to the Holy Mosque[54] as long as heaven and earth will exist, to the journey of the Messenger of Allah,[55] be Allah's peace and blessing upon him, to it, and to his ascension from it.[56]

"Dwelling one day in the Path of Allah is better than the entire world and everything that exists in it. The place of the whip of one among you in paradise is better than the entire world and everything that exists in it. [God's] worshiper's going and coming in the Path of Allah is better than the entire world and everything that exists in it." (*Told by Bukhari, Muslim Tirmidhi and Ibn Maja*).[57]

I swear by that who holds in His Hands the Soul of Muhammad! I indeed wish to go to war for the sake of Allah! I will assault and kill, assault and kill, assault and kill (*told by Bukhari and Muslim*).[58]

Article Sixteen

We must accord the Islamic [young] generations in our area an Islamic education based on the implementation of religious precepts, on the conscientious study of the Book of Allah; on the study of the prophetic tradition,[59] on the study of Islamic history and heritage from its reliable sources, under the guidance of experts and scientists,[60] and on singling out the paths which constitute for the Muslims sound concepts of thinking and faith. It is also necessary to study conscientiously the enemy and its material and human potential; to detect its weak and strong spots, and to recognize the powers that support it and stand by it. At the same time, we must be aware of current events, follow the news and study the analyses and commentaries on it, together with drawing plans for the present and the future and examining every phenomenon, so that every Muslim, fighting *jihad*, could live out his era aware of his objective, his goals, his way and the things happening around him.

"O my dear son! Lo! though it be but the weight of a grain of mustard seed, and though it be in a rock, or in the heavens, or in the earth, Allah will bring it forth. Lo! Allah is subtle. Aware. O my dear son! Establish worship and enjoin kindness and forbid inequity, and persevere, whatever may befall thee. Lo! that is of the steadfast heart of things. Turn not thy cheek in scorn toward folk, nor walk with pertness in the land. Lo! Allah loves not braggarts and boasters." *Sura XXXI (Luqman), verses 16-18.*

The Role of Muslim Women

Article Seventeen

The Muslim women have a no lesser role than that of men in the war of liberation; they manufacture men and play a great role in guiding and educating the [new] generation. The enemies have understood that role, therefore they realize that if they can guide and educate [the Muslim women] in a way that would distance them from Islam, they would have won that war. Therefore, you can see them making consistent efforts [in that direction] by way of publicity and movies, curricula of education and culture, using as their intermediaries their craftsmen who are part of the various Zionist organizations which take on all sorts of names and shapes such as: the Freemasons, Rotary Clubs, gangs of spies and the like. All of them are nests of saboteurs and sabotage.Those Zionist organizations control vast material resources, which enable them to fulfill their mission amidst societies, with a view of implementing Zionist goals and sowing the concepts that can be of use to the enemy. Those organizations operate [in a situation] where Islam is absent from the arena and alienated from its people. Thus, the Muslims must fulfill their duty in confronting the schemes of those saboteurs. When Islam will retake possession of [the means to] guide the life [of the Muslims], it will wipe out those organizations which are the enemy of humanity and Islam.

Article Eighteen

The women in the house and the family of *jihad* fighters, whether they are mothers or sisters, carry out the most important duty of caring for the home and raising the children upon the moral concepts and values which derive from Islam; and of educating their sons to observe the religious injunctions in preparation for the duty of *jihad* awaiting them. Therefore, we must pay attention to the schools and curricula upon which Muslim girls are educated, so as to make them righteous mothers, who are conscious of their duties in the war of liberation. They must be fully capable of being aware and of grasping the ways to manage their households. Economy and avoiding waste in household expenditures are prerequisites to our ability to pursue our cause in the difficult circumstances surrounding us. Therefore let them remember at all times that money saved is equivalent to blood, which must be made to run in the veins in order to ensure the continuity of life of our young and old.

"Lo, men who surrender unto Allah and women who surrender, and men who believe and women who believe, and men who obey and women who obey, and men who speak the truth and women who speak the truth, and men who persevere, (in righteousness) and women who persevere, and men who are humble and women who are humble, and men who give alms and women who give alms, and men who fast and women who fast, and men who guard their modesty and women who guard [their modesty], and men who remember Allah much and women who remember Allah has prepared for them forgiveness and a vast reward." *Sura 33 (Al-Ahzab, the Clans), verse 35.*

The Role of Islamic Art in the War of Liberation

Article Nineteen

Art has rules and criteria by which one can know whether it is Islamic or Jahiliyya[61] art. The problems of Islamic liberation underlie the need for Islamic art which could lift the spirit, and instead of making one party triumph over the other, would lift up all parties in harmony and balance.

Man is a strange and miraculous being, made out of a handful of clay and a breath of soul; Islamic art is to address man on this basis,

145

while Jahili art addresses the body and makes the element of clay paramount. So, books, articles, publications, religious exhortations, epistles, songs, poems, hymns, plays, and the like, if they possess the characteristics of Islamic art, have the requisites of ideological mobilization, of a continuous nurturing in the pursuance of the journey, and of relaxing the soul. The road is long and the suffering is great and the spirits are weary; it is Islamic art which renews the activity, revives the movement and arouses lofty concepts and sound planning. The soul cannot thrive, unless it knows how to contrive, unless it can transit from one situation to another. All this is a serious matter, no jesting. For the *umma*[62] fighting its *jihad* knows no jesting.

Social Solidarity

Article Twenty

Islamic society is one of solidarity. The Messenger of Allah, be Allah's prayer and peace upon him, said:

What a wonderful tribe were the Ash'aris! When they were overtaxed, either in their location or during their journeys, they would collect all their possessions, and then would divide them equally among themselves.

This is the Islamic spirit which ought to prevail in any Muslim society. A society which confronts a vicious, Nazi-like enemy, who does not differentiate between man and woman, elder and young, ought to be the first to adorn itself with this Islamic spirit. Our enemy pursues the style of collective punishment, of usurping people's countries and properties, of pursuing them into their exiles[63] and places of assembly. It has resorted to breaking bones, opening fire on women and children and the old, with or without reason, and to setting up detention camps where thousands upon thousands are interned in inhuman conditions. In addition, it destroys houses, renders children orphans, and issues oppressive judgements against thousands of young people who spend the best years of their youth in the darkness of prisons. The Nazism of the Jews does not skip women and children, it scares everyone. They make war against people's livelihood, plunder their moneys and threaten their honor. In their horrible actions they mistreat people like the most horrendous war criminals. Exiling people from their country is another way of killing them. As we face this misconduct, we have no escape from establishing social solidarity among the people, from confronting the enemy as one solid body, so that if one organ is hurt the rest of the body will respond with alertness and fervor.

Article Twenty-One

Social solidarity consists of extending help to all the needy, both materially and morally, or assisting in the execution of certain actions. It is incumbent upon the members of the Hamas to look after the interests of the masses the way they would look after their own interests. They must spare no effort in the implementation and maintenance of those interests, and they must avoid playing with anything that might effect the future generations or cause damage to their society. For the masses are of them and for them, their strength is [ultimately] theirs and their future is theirs. The members of Hamas must share with the people its joys and sorrows, and adopt the demands of the people and anything likely to fulfill its interests and theirs. When this spirit reigns, congeniality will deepen, cooperation and compassion will prevail, unity will firm up, and the ranks will be strengthened in the confrontation with the enemy.

The Powers which Support the Enemy

Article Twenty-Two

The enemies have been scheming for a long time, and they have consolidated their schemes, in order to achieve what they have achieved. They took advantage of key elements in unfolding events, and accumulated a huge and influential material wealth which they put to the service of implementing their dream. This wealth [permitted them to] take over control of the world media such as news agencies, the press, publication houses, broadcasting and the like. [They also used this] wealth to stir revolutions in various parts of the globe in order to fulfill their interests and pick the fruits. They stood behind the French and the Communist revolutions and behind most of the revolutions we hear about here and there. They also used the money to establish clandestine organizations which are spreading around the world, in order to destroy societies and carry out Zionist interests. Such organizations are: the Freemasons, Rotary Clubs, Lions Clubs, B'nai B'rith and the like. All of them are destructive spying organizations. They also used the money to take over control of the imperialist states and made them colonize many countries in order to exploit the wealth of those countries and spread their corruption therein.

As regards local and world wars, it has come to pass and no one objects, that they stood behind World War I, so as to wipe out the Islamic Caliphate.[64] They collected material gains and took control of many sources of wealth. They obtained the Balfour Declaration[65] and established the League of Nations in order to rule the world by means of that organization. They also stood behind World War II, where they collected immense benefits from trading with war materials and prepared for the establishment of their state. They inspired the establishment of the United Nations and the Security Council to replace the League of Nations, in order to rule the world by their intermediary. There was no war that broke out anywhere without their fingerprints on it:

"...As often as they light a fire for war, Allah extinguishes it. Their efforts are for corruption in the land and Allah loves not corrupters." *Sura V (Al-Ma'ida, the Tablespread), verse 64.*[65]

The forces of imperialism in both the capitalist West and the Communist East support the enemy with all their might, in material and human terms, taking turns between themselves. When Islam appears, all the forces of unbelief unite to confront it, because the community of unbelief is one.

"Oh ye who believe! Take not for intimates others than your own folk, who would spare no pain to ruin you. Hatred is revealed by [the utterance of] their mouth, but that which their breasts hide is greater. We have made plain for you the revelations if you will understand." *Sura III (Al-Imran), verse 118.*

It is not in vain that the verse ends with God's saying: "If you will understand."

Part IV

Our Position vis-a-vis the Islamic Movements

Article Twenty-Three

The Hamas views the other Islamic movements with respect and appreciation. Even when it differs from them in one aspect or another or on one concept or another, it agrees with them in other aspects and concepts. It reads those movements as included in the framework of striving [for the sake of Allah], as long as they hold sound intentions and abide by their devotion to Allah, and as along as their conduct remains within the perimeter of the Islamic circle. All the fighters of *jihad* have their reward.

The Hamas regards those movements as its stockholders and asks Allah for guidance and integrity of conduct for all. It shall not fail to continue to raise the banner of unity and to exert efforts in order to implement it, [based] upon the [Holy] Book and the [Prophet's] Tradition.[67]

"And hold fast, all of you together, to the cable of Allah, do not separate. And remember Allah's favor unto you how ye were enemies and He made friendship between your hearts so that ye became as brothers by His grace; and (how) ye were upon the brink of an abyss of fire, and He did save you from it. Thus Allah makes clear His revelations unto you, that happily ye may be guided." *Sura III (Al-'Imran), verse 102.*[68]

Article Twenty-Four

The Hamas will not permit the slandering and defamation of individuals and groups, for the Believers are not slanderers and cursers.[69] However, despite the need to differentiate between that and the positions and modes of conduct adopted by individuals and groups whenever the Hamas detects faulty positions and modes of conduct, it has the right to point to the mistake, to denigrate it, to act for spelling out the truth and for adopting it realistically in the context of a given problem. Wisdom is roaming around, and the Believer ought to grasp it wherever he can find it.

"Allah loves not the utterance of harsh speech save by one who has been wronged. Allah is ever Hearer, Knower. If you do good openly or keep it secret, or give evil, lo! Allah is forgiving, powerful." *Sura IV (Women), verses 147-148.*[70]

The National (Wataniyya) Movements in the Palestinian Arena

Article Twenty-Five

[The Hamas] reciprocated its respect to them, appreciates their condition and the factors surrounding them and influencing them, and supports them firmly as long as they do not owe their loyalty to the Communist East or to the Crusader West. We reiterate to everyone who is part of them or sympathizes with them that the Hamas is a movement of *jihad*, or morality and consciousness in its concept of life. It moves forward with the others, abhors opportunism, and only wishes well to individuals and groups. It does not aspire to material gains, or to personal fame, nor does it solicit remuneration from the people. It sets out relying on its own material resources, and what is available to it, [as it is said] "afford them the power you can avail yourself of." [All that] in order to carry out its duty, to gain Allah's favor; it has no ambition other than that.

All the nationalist streams, operating in the Palestinian arena for the sake of the liberation of Palestine, may rest assured that they will definitely and resolutely get support and assistance, in speech and in action, at the present and in the future, [because the Hamas aspires] to unite, not to divide; to safeguard, not to squander; to bring together, not to fragment. It values every kind word, every devoted effort and every commendable endeavor. It closes the door before marginal quarrels, it does not heed rumors and biased statements, and it is aware of the right of self-defense.

Anything that runs counter or contradicts this orientation is trumped up by the enemies or by those who run in their orbit in order to create confusion, to divide our ranks or to divert to marginal things.

"O ye who believe! If an evil-liver bring you tidings,[71] verify it, lest ye smite some folk in ignorance and afterward repent of what ye did." *Sura XLIX (al Hujurat, the Private Apartments), verse 6.*

Article Twenty-Six

The Hamas, while it views positively the Palestinian national movements which do not owe their loyalty to the East or to the West, does not refrain from debating unfolding events regarding the Palestinian problem on the local and international scenes. These debates are realistic and expose the extent to which [these developments] go along with, or contradict, national interests as viewed from the Islamic vantage point.

The Palestine Liberation Organization

Article Twenty-Seven

The PLO is among the closest to the Hamas, for it constitutes a father, a brother, a relative, a friend. Can a Muslim turn away from his father, his brother, his relative or his friend? Our homeland is one, our calamity is one, our destiny is one and our enemy is common to both of us. Under the influence of the circumstances which surrounded the founding of the PLO, and the ideological invasion which has swept the Arab world since the rout of the Crusades, and which has been reinforced by orientalism and the Christian mission, the PLO has adopted the idea of a secular state, and so we think of it. Secular thought is diametrically opposed to religious thought. Thought is the basis for positions, for modes of conduct and for resolutions. Therefore, in spite of our appreciation for the PLO and its possible transformation in the future, and despite the fact that we do not denigrate its role in the Arab-Israeli conflict, we cannot substitute it for the Islamic nature of Palestine by adopting secular thought. For the Islamic nature of Palestine is part of our religion, and anyone who neglects his religion is bound to lose.

"And who forsakes the religion of Abraham, save him who befools himself?" *Sura II (Al-Baqra, the Cow), verse 130.*

When the PLO adopts Islam as the guideline for life, then we shall become its soldiers, the fuel of its fire which will burn the enemies. And until that happens, and we pray to Allah that it will happen soon, the position of the Hamas towards the PLO is one of a son towards his father, a brother towards his brother, and a relative towards his relative, who suffers the other's pain when a thorn hits him, who supports the other in the confrontation with the enemies and who wishes him divine guidance and integrity of conduct.

Your brother, your brother! Whoever has no brother is like a fighter who runs to the battle without weapons. A cousin for man is like the best wing, and no falcon can take off without wings.

Article Twenty-Eight

The Zionist invasion is a mischievous one. It does not hesitate to take any road, or to pursue all despicable and repulsive means to fulfill its desires. It relies to a great extent, for its meddling and spying activities, on the clandestine organizations which it has established, such as the Freemasons, Rotary Clubs, Lions, and other spying associations. All those secret organizations, some of which are overt, act for the interests of Zionism and, under its directions, strive to demolish societies, to destroy values, to wreck answerableness,[72] to totter virtues and to wipe out Islam. It stands behind the diffusion of drugs and toxics of all kinds in order to facilitate its control and expansion.

The Arab states surrounding Israel are required to open their borders to the *jihad* fighters, the sons of the Arab and Islamic peoples, to enable them to play their role and to join their efforts to those of their brothers among the Muslim Brothers in Palestine.

The other Arab and Islamic states are required, at the very least, to facilitate the movement of the *jihad* fighters to and from them. We cannot fail to remind every Muslim that when the Jews occupied Holy Jerusalem in 1967 and stood at the doorstep of the Blessed Aqsa Mosque, they shouted with joy: "Muhammad is dead, he left daughters behind."[73]

Israel, by virtue of its being Jewish and of having a Jewish population, defies Islam and the Muslims.

"Let the eyes of the cowards not fall asleep."

National and Religious Associations, Institutions, the Intelligentsia, and the Arab and Islamic Worlds

Article Twenty-Nine

The Hamas hopes that those associations will stand by it on all levels, will support it, adopt its positions, boost its activities and moves and encourage support for it, so as to render the Islamic people its backers and helpers, and its strategic depth in all human and material domains as well as in information, in time and space. Among other things, they hold solidarity meetings, issue explanatory publications, supportive articles and tendentious leaflets to make the masses aware of the Palestinian issue, the problems it faces, and of the plans to resolve them; and to mobilize the Islamic peoples ideologically, educationally and culturally in order to fulfill their role in the crucial war of liberation, as they had played their role in the defeat of the Crusades and in the rout of the Tartars and had saved human civilization. How all that is dear to Allah!

"Allah has decreed: Lo! I verily shall conquer, I and my messengers. Lo! Allah is strong, Almighty." *Sura LVIII (Al-Mujadilah), verse 21.*

Article Thirty

Men of letters, members of the intelligentsia, media people, preachers, teachers and educators, and all different sectors in the Arab and Islamic world are all called upon to play their role and to carry out their duty in view of the wickedness of the Zionist invasion, of its penetration into many countries, and its control over material means and the media, with all the ramifications thereof in most countries of the world.

Jihad means not only carrying arms and denigrating the enemies. Uttering positive words, writing good articles and useful books, and lending support and assistance, all that too is *jihad* in the path of Allah, as long as intentions are sincere to make Allah's banner supreme.

"Those who prepare for a raid in the path of Allah are considered as if they participated themselves in the raid. Those who successfully rear a raider in their home are considered as if they participated themselves in the raid." (*Told by Bukhari, Muslim, Abu Dawud and Tirmidhi*).

The Members of Other Religions; The Hamas is a Humane Movement

Article Thirty-One

The Hamas is a humane movement, which cares for human rights and is committed to the tolerance inherent in Islam as regards attitudes towards other religions. It is only hostile to those who are hostile towards it, or stand in its way in order to disturb its moves or to frustrate its efforts.

Under the shadow of Islam it is possible for the members of the three religions: Islam, Christianity and Judaism, to coexist in safety and security. Safety and security can only prevail under the shadow of Islam, and recent and ancient history is the best witness to that effect. The members of other religions must desist from struggling against Islam over sovereignty in this region. For if they were to gain the upper hand, fighting, torture and uprooting would follow; they would be fed up with each other, to say nothing of members of other religions. The past and the present are full of evidence to that effect.

"They will not fight you in body safe in fortified villages or from behind walls. Their adversity among themselves is very great. Ye think of them as a whole whereas their hearts are diverse. That is because they are a folk who have no sense." *Sura 59 (al-Hashr, the Exile), verse 14.*

Islam accords his rights to everyone who has rights and averts aggression against the rights of others. The Nazi Zionist practices against our people will not last the lifetime of their invasion, for "states built upon oppression last only one hour, states based upon justice will last until the hour of Resurrection."

"Allah forbids you not those who warred not against you on account of religion and drove you not out from your houses, that you should show them kindness and deal justly with them. Lo! Allah loves the just dealers." *Sura 60 (Al-Mumtahana), verse 8.*

154

The Attempts to Isolate the Palestinian People

Article Thirty-Two

World Zionism and imperialist forces have been attempting, with smart moves and considered planning, to push the Arab countries, one after another, out of the circle of conflict with Zionism, in order, ultimately, to isolate the Palestinian people. Egypt has already been cast out of the conflict, to a very great extent through the treacherous Camp David Accords, and she has been trying to drag other countries into similar agreements in order to push them out of the circle of conflict.

The Hamas is calling upon the Arab and Islamic peoples to act seriously and tirelessly in order to frustrate that dreadful scheme and to make the masses aware of the danger of withdrawing from the circle of struggle with Zionism. Today it is Palestine and tomorrow it may be another country or other countries. For Zionist scheming has no end, and after Palestine they will covet expansion from the Nile to the Euphrates. Only when they have completed digesting the area on which they will have laid their hand, they will look forward to more expansion, etc. Their scheme has been laid out in the *Protocols of the Elders of Zion*, and their present [conduct] is the best proof of what is said there.

Leaving the circle of conflict with Israel is a major act of treason and it will bring a curse on its perpetrators.

"Who so on that day turns his back to them, unless maneuvering for battle or intent to join a company, he truly has incurred wrath from Allah, and his habitation will be hell, a hapless journey's end." *Sura 8 (al-Anfal, Spoils of War), verse 16.*

We have no escape from pooling together all the forces and energies to face this despicable Nazi-Tatar invasion. Otherwise we shall witness the loss of [our] countries, the uprooting of their inhabitants, the spreading of corruption on earth and the destruction of all religious values. Let everyone realize that he is accountable to Allah.

"Whoever does a speck of good will bear [the consequences] and whoever does a speck of evil will see [the consequences]."

Within the circle of the conflict with world Zionism, the Hamas regards itself the spearhead and the avant-garde. It joins its efforts to all those who are active on the Palestinian scene, but more steps

155

need to be taken by the Arab and Islamic peoples and Islamic associations throughout the Arab and Islamic world in order to make possible the next round with the Jews,[74] the merchants of war.

"We have cast among them enmity and hatred till the day of Resurrection. As often as they light a fire for war, Allah extinguishes it. Their effort is for corruption in the land, and Allah loves not corrupters." *Sura V (Al-Ma'idah, the Table Spread), verse 64.*[75]

Article Thirty-Three

The Hamas sets out from these general concepts which are consistent and in accordance with the rules of the universe, and gushes forth in the river of fate in its confrontation and *jihad* waging against the enemies, in defense of the Muslim human being, of Islamic civilization and of the Islamic Holy Places, primarily the blessed Aqsa Mosque. This, for the purpose of calling upon the Arab and Islamic peoples as well as their governments, popular and official associations, to fear Allah in their attitude towards and dealings with the Hamas, and to be, in accordance with Allah's will, its supporters and partisans who extend assistance to it and provide it with reinforcement after reinforcement, until the Decree of Allah is fulfilled, the ranks are over-swollen, *jihad* fighters join other *jihad* fighters, and all this accumulation sets out from everywhere in the Islamic world, obeying the call of duty, and intoning "Come on, join *jihad*!" This call will tear apart the clouds in the skies and it will continue to ring until liberation is completed, the invaders are vanquished, and Allah's victory sets in.

"Verily Allah helps one who helps Him. Lo! Allah is strong, Almighty." *Sura XXII (Pilgrimage), verse 40.*

Part V — The Testimony of History

Confronting Aggressors Throughout History

Article Thirty-Four

Palestine is the navel of the earth, the convergence of continents, the object of greed for the greedy, since the dawn of history. The Prophet, may Allah's prayer and peace be upon him, points out to that fact in his noble *hadith*[76] in which he implored his venerable companion, Ma'adh ibn Jabl, saying:

"O Ma'adh, Allah is going to grant you victory over Syria after me, from Al-Arish to the Euphrates, while its men, women, and female slaves will be dwelling there until the Day of Resurrection. Those of you who chose [to dwell in] one of the plains of Syria or Palestine[77] will be in a state of *jihad* to the Day of Resurrection." The greedy have coveted Palestine more than once and they raided it with armies in order to fulfill their covetousness. Multitudes of Crusades descended on it, carrying their faith with them and waving their Cross. They were able to defeat the Muslims for a long time, and the Muslims were not able to redeem it until they sought the protection of their religious banner; then, they unified their forces, sang the praise of their God and set out for *jihad* under the command of Saladin al-Ayyubi, for the duration of nearly two decades, and then the obvious conquest took place when the Crusaders were defeated and Palestine was liberated.[78]

"Say (O Muhammad) unto those who disbelieve: ye shall be overcome and gathered unto Hell, an evil resting place." *Sura III (Al-Imran), verse 12.*

This is the only way to liberation, there is no doubt in the testimony of history. That is one of the rules of the universe and one of the laws of existence. Only iron can blunt iron, only the true faith of Islam can vanquish their false and falsified faith. Faith can only be fought by faith. Ultimately, victory is reserved to the truth, and truth is victorious.

"And verily our word went forth of old unto our bordmen sent [to warn]. That they verily would be helped. And that our host, they verily would be the victors." *Sura 38 (Al-Saffat), verses 171-3.*

Article Thirty-Five

The Hamas takes a serious look at the defeat of the Crusades at the hand of Saladin the Ayyubid and the rescue of Palestine from their domination; at the defeat of the Tatars at Ein Jalut[79] where their spine was broken by Qutuz[80] and Al-Dhahir Baibars,[81] and the Arab world was rescued from the sweep of the Tatars which ruined all aspects of human civilization. The Hamas has learned from these lessons and examples that the current Zionist invasion had been preceded by a Crusader invasion from the West; and another one, the Tatars, from the East. And exactly as the Muslims had faced those invasions and planned their removal and defeat, they are able to face the Zionist invasion and defeat it. This will not be difficult for Allah if our intentions are pure and our determination is sincere; if the Muslims draw useful lessons from the experiences of the past, and extricate themselves for the vestiges of the [Western] ideological onslaught; and if they follow the traditions of Islam.

Epilogue

The Hamas are Soldiers

Article Thirty-Six

The Hamas, while breaking its path, reiterates time and again to all members of our people and the Arab and Islamic peoples, that it does not seek fame for itself nor material gains, nor social status. Nor is it directed against any one member of our people in order to compete with him or replace him. There is nothing of that at all. It will never set out against any Muslims or against the non-Muslims who make peace with it, here or anywhere else. It will only be of help to all associations and organizations which act against the Zionist enemy and those who revolve in its orbit.

The Hamas posits Islam as a way of life, it is its faith and its yardstick for judging. Whoever posits Islam as a way of life, anywhere, and regardless of whether it is an organization, a state, or any other group, the Hamas are its soldiers, nothing else.

158

We implore Allah to guide us, to guide through us and to decide between us and our folk with truth.

"Our Lord! Decide with truth between us and our folk, for Thou are the best of those who make decisions." *Sura VII (Al-A'raf, the Heights), verse 89.*

Our last call is: Thanks to Allah, the Lord of the Universe.

* * *

Author's Epilogue

As this manuscript goes to press, the intifada is still raging and no prospects for an early settlement are in sight. The Hamas' role in the intifada is on the rise, so much so that it not only challenges the monopoly of the PLO on the leadership of the unrest, but it has been shaping its own modes of rebellion against Israel. They have been issuing their own announcements calling for strikes and other measures, they have their own network of leaders and activists, and they seem to make a deeper dent on public opinion as the political impasse leads nowhere and as the PLO leadership does not deliver anything beyond rhetoric. The mass arrests in May 1989 of the Hamas leadership in the Gaza Strip, including its charismatic head Sheikh Yasin, do not seem to have significantly blunted the appeal of the movement.

Announcement No. 29 of the movement, published and distributed in the West Bank on September 5, 1988, is one of the most illustrative of all the Hamas' messages which had been published until and since then. On the occasion of the beginning of the tenth month of the intifada, the announcement called upon the people of the territories:

a) To pursue its struggle against its enemies, the "Nazi Jews,"[82] who have adopted all possible means against the Palestinians, such as: killing, exile, breaking bones, aggression against holy places and mosques, arrests, hostile acts against properties, robbery of funds, publication of false and forged[83] facts, and drawing slogans on walls in order to pit one party against another.

b) The "Nazi Jews" have uprooted the Palestinian people and usurped its rights. They stand behind all massacres and disasters which have befallen the Palestinian people. Sometimes they act directly against the Palestinians, at other times via their agents. Not

159

long ago, the Palestinian people suffered the tragedy of Sabra and Shatilla[84] on September 17, 1982. What happened to our families there is still a fresh memory.

c) On the anniversary of the arson of the Aqsa Mosque[85] the Hamas is calling its members to a general strike. Despite the efforts of the Jews to break the general strike, the Palestinian people, who entertain their anger against the Jews, will not submit.

d) The Hamas does not act against the people, its reputation or its property. It is only set against the Jews and their aides. Those who spread false humors against the Hamas are imposters and liars.[86]

e) Therefore, the Hamas announces a general strike to commemorate the three following dates:

1. September 9, the beginning of the tenth month of the intifada.

2. September 18, the massacres of Sabra and Shatilla.

3. September 26, the conquest of Khaybar.[87] This is a day of resistance when we will hit the Jews whenever and wherever possible in order to achieve our liberty, rid ourselves of occupation and retrieve our rights.[88]

The announcement ends with the exhortation that "those who challenge Allah will be condemned to misery," an obvious reference to Jews.

Notes

* As translated, interpreted and annotated by this author. This chapter first appeared in Y. Alexander and H. Foxman, eds., *The 1988-1989 Annual on Terrorism* (The Netherlands: Kluwer Academic Publishers), pp. 99-134.

1. See S. Lachman, "Arab Rebellion and Terrorism in Palestine 1929-1939," in *Zionism and Arabism in Palestine and Israel*, E. Kedourie and S. Haim, eds., (London: Frank Cass, 1982), pp. 52-99. See also Nels Johnson, *Islam and the Politics of Meaning in Palestinian Nationalism* (London: Kegan Paul, 1982), pp. 38-44.

2. A. Cohen, *Political Parties in the West Bank under the Jordanian Regime 1949-1967* (Ithaca: Cornell University Press, 1982), p. 144.

3. Th. Mayer, "The Military Force of Islam: The Society of the Muslim Brothers and the Palestine Question 1945-8," in Kedourie and Haim, eds., *Zionism and Arabism in Palestine and Israel*, p. 101.

4. M. Shadid, "The Muslim Brotherhood Movement in the West Bank and Gaza," *Third World Quarterly*, Vol. 10, No. 2 (1988): 659.

5. *Ibid.*, p. 661. See also Cohen, *op. cit.*, pp. 148-51.

6. Shadid, p. 660.

7. *Ibid.*

8. Johnson, *Islam and the Politics of Meaning*, pp. 8-15.

9. *Ibid.*

10. *Ibid.*, pp. 74-87.

11. See Y. Litani's article in *Haaretz* of 18 January 1982; and P. Johnson and J. Tucker, "Political Islam and the West Bank," *MERIP Reports* (February 1982): 15-17.

12. Shadid, *op. cit.* See also A. Lesch and M. Tessler, "The West Bank and Gaza: Political and Ideological Response to Occupation," *The Muslim World*, Vol. 77, No. 3-4 (July-October 1987): 229-249.

13. For the usages of the political language of Islam, see B. Lewis' insightful study: *The Political Language of Islam* (Chicago: University of Chicago, 1988).

14. These estimates are based on interviews that were conducted by Israeli and other journalists in the territories. No conclusive data exist in this regard.

15. Hamas, the acronym for the Islamic Resistance Movement (*Harakat Muqawama Islamiyya*), literally means "enthusiasm," "zeal," "fanaticism," which is quite descriptive of their mode of operation.

16. This is the classical Muslim designation for Jews and Christians whose scriptures had been acknowledged by Islam, except that they were accused of having forged parts of their holy texts, thus making the divine message of the Qur'an, which supplanted them, an updated imperative.

17. This means that unless the Scriptuary peoples (specifically the Jews) grasp and keep the Covenant which the Prophet had made with them in Medinah, ignominy shall be their fate.

18. Translation follows Muhammad Marmaduke Pickthall's *The Meaning of the Glorious Koran* (New York: Mentor Books, n.d.). According to this translation, the verses in question are 110-112.

19. Hassan al-Banna was the founder of the Muslim Brothers in Egypt in the 1920s. The Hamas claim affiliation with that movement.

20. *Da'wa* is the "call," the "Mission," which successive Islamic movements have used as a euphemism for their indoctrination and missionary set-up. The journal of the Muslim Brothers in Egypt is also called *Da'wa*.

21. Holy War for the cause of Islam.

22. *Fath* is used here in the traditional Islamic sense of conquest by and for the sake of Islam. Hence the sanctity of the conquered land as part of *Dar-al-Islam*, the Abode of Islam.

23. Palestine was conquered by Umar ibn al-Khattab, one of the Prophet's closest and ablest companions and the second Caliph of Islam (634-644).

24. The translation of the verse is Pickthall's, *op. cit.*

25. Under Islam, Jews (and other Scriptuaries for that matter) are indeed assured the status of *Ahl-a-dhimma* (protected people), which guarantees their lives and property as long as they submit to the rule of Islam, pay the poll-tax (*jizya*) and conform to the restrictions imposed upon them by Islamic rule.

26. A prominent Indian-Muslim thinker and theologian.

27. See the Author's Introduction for the context of Qassam's role in Palestine in the 1930s.

28. In the 1948 War of Israel's Independence, the Muslim Brothers played a meaningful role. See the Author's Introduction.

29. During the War of Attrition which followed the Arab defeat of 1967, groups of the Muslim Brothers purportedly participated in attacks against Israel.

30. Reference is made to the Day of Judgement. This tradition (*hadith*), which is imputed to the Prophet, has been often quoted in Islamic literature, old and modern. The Egyptian troops who launched the

assault on the Bar-Lev Line in October 1973, were equipped with "booklets of guidance" which included, inter alia, this same quotation.

31. Some sort of desert tree, probably the wild orache.

32. Bukhari and Muslim are the authors of the two most authoritative and widely accepted collections of *hadith* (traditions of the Prophet).

33. *Waqf* is a religious endowment. There are various kinds: family and private *waqfs*, whose proceeds accrue to the members of the donor's family, and after the death of the last descendant go to a charitable purpose; public endowments set apart for a charitable or religious purpose. The Holy Land is regarded, like all lands conquered forcibly by Islam, as inalienable property belonging to the Muslim public.

34. *Shari'a* is the Holy Law of Islam.

35. The Second Caliph of Islam (634-644) after the death of the Prophet. Under his reign the Islamic Empire, including Palestine, was established and expanded.

36. "*Raqba*" in Arabic could mean either control, supervision, guardianship, or could be read "*raqaba,*" meaning the slaves working on the land.

37. In Pickthall's version, it is verses 95-96.

38. On the meaning of *watan* and *wataniyya,* see the Author's Introduction.

39. *Fard 'ayn* is an individual duty under Islamic law, as distinguished from *Fard kifaya*, which is a collective duty. *Fard 'ayn* is an absolute duty which overrides other considerations such as the duties of a wife towards her husband and of a slave towards his master.

40. It is significant that the first sentence of this verse: "There is no compulsion in religion," which the Muslims often cite as a proof of tolerance in Islam, was dropped from this quotation, indicating the absolute, unshared and uncompromising truth of Islam, the "right direction."

41. The heads of the Hamas, notably Sheikh Yasin of Gaza, when interviewed by the media on their solution to the Palestinian problem, have termed diplomatic demarches as a "waste of time."

42. This is an allusion to the traditional Islamic method of scholarly examination of *hadiths* of the Prophet in order to ascertain their veracity.

43. Jerusalem was declared by the Prophet as the Qibla (direction of prayer) for the Believers in Medinah, apparently as a gesture towards the Jews there, whom he hoped to convert to his faith. However, after he broke with the Jews, and when he conquered Mecca, this became the Qibla of all Muslims. But Jerusalem retained its exalted title as the First Qibla.

44. The two holiest shrines of Islam are in Mecca, where the Black Stone of the Ka'ba is located, and Medinah where the Prophet lived and died. Third in line is the Haram-al-sharif on the Temple Mount in Jerusalem where the Prophet is believed to have ascended to the Seven Heavens (*Mi'raj*).

45. The *Masra* is the point of departure for the Prophet's journey to the heavens.

46. This is recognized in Islamic tradition as Mecca.

47. The "far-distant place," in Arabic *Al-Aqsa*, has been referred to Jerusalem by Islamic tradition, hence the Aqsa Mosque is located on the purported spot of Muhammad's visit.

48. This Sura is also known as the "Children of Israel."

49. See footnote 39 above.

50. See footnote 39 above.

51. Salah-a-din, or Saladin, a Muslim Kurd who ruled the Ayyubid Kingdom at the time of the Crusaders, has become renowned after the defeat he inflicted on the Crusaders in the decisive Hittin Battle (1187) and his second conquest of Jerusalem for Islam (1189). In the modern world of Islam his memory has been revived and cultivated as part of the struggle against Zionism, which is usually likened, in contemporary Arab/Muslim literature, to the medieval Crusades.

52. General Allenby took over Palestine from the Ottomans during World War I, to usher in the era of the British Mandate over Palestine which lasted until 1948. No reference could be found by the author to anything said by the British General relating his takeover of Jerusalem with the Crusades.

53. The Arabic original speaks about General "Guru," which is probably a rendering of General Gouraud, the first French High Commissioner in Syria, who is reputed to have uttered that statement.

54. According to Islamic tradition, this was the place of the Prophet's point of departure for his journey from Mecca to Jerusalem. See footnotes 40-45 above.

55. See footnote 44 above.

56. See footnotes 43-45 above.

57. On *hadith* collectors and transmitters, see footnote 32 above.

58. See footnote 32 above.

59. Reliance on the Qur'an and the *Sunna* (tradition of the Prophet) is characteristic of fundamentalist Islamic movements, who hold in low esteem the other three of the *Usul-a-Din* (the Foundation of the Faith, the sources of the Shari'a law), namely *Qiyas* (analogy), *Ijma'* (consensus) and *Ada* (local customs).

60. Scientists here are *Ahl-al-Ilm-ulama* (the Doctors of the Holy Law).

61. *Jahiliyya* is the era of ignorance which preceded the coming of the Prophet Muhammad, an era usually depicted in terms of oppression, lawlessness, ungodliness, injustice and darkness, until the prophetic message of Muhammad brought light unto the Arabs of Arabia. Thereafter, any reversion to anti-Islamic or a-Islamic rule, any renegation of Islam or act of apostasy by Muslims in all domains of life, have been described by Islamic fundamentalist literature as a return to *Jahiliyya*.

62. The *umma* is the universal congregation of all Muslims.

63. Reference is made to Israel's occasional actions among Palestinian populations across its borders.

64. The dismemberment of the Ottoman Empire indeed signalled the end of the Caliphate.

65. The famous letter of Lord Balfour, the British Foreign Secretary, dated 2 November 1917, in which he pledged Britain's help to establish a Jewish Homeland in Palestine, which was to be given as a mandate to the British after the war.

66. This is only part of the verse which refers specifically to the Jews and says, inter alia, "we have cast among them enmity and hatred till the Day of Resurrection."

67. See footnote 59 above.

68. In Pickthall's translation, it is verse 103.

69. In view of what was said above about the Jews, as individuals and as a group, it appears that they are the exception to this rule.

70. In Pickthall's translation, they are verses 148-9.

71. The reference is to a man who brought false news of a revolt of the subject Jews at Khaybar.

72. The term used is *dhimam*, the plural of *dhimma*, the very word in Islamic tradition which defined the status of Jews (and Christians) under Islam. These people were protected and safe if they paid a special capital tax and recognized the hegemony of Islam.

73. It is impossible to ascertain what this claim is based on. There is a popular Arabic song which denigrated those who failed to rear sons and only left behind daughters.

74. Despite their protestations to the contrary, the Hamas uses Jews and Zionism interchangeably. The thrust of their assault is against Zionism, but by introducing incidentally antisemitic themes, such as the *Protocols of the Elders of Zion*, which preceded the birth of Zionism, they expose their real intent against Jews in general.

75. This verse explicitly talks about the Jews in its first part which is not quoted here.

76. A tradition related to the Prophet and indicating that he did or said or approved of a particular thing. Since the Prophet is taken to be the most noble of men and his life is a model to be emulated, knowing the

hadith and acting upon it is regarded as one of the loftiest pursuits in Islam.

77. The term used is *Bayt al-maqdas*, the Holy House. This term was used to denominate Jerusalem and then, by extension, all Palestine.

78. See footnote 51.

79. The battle of Ein Jalut (1260) is one that arrested the advance of the Mongols in the Middle East when they were defeated by the Muslim Mameluks under Baibars (1223-1277).

80. A Mameluk king of Egypt (1259-1260).

81. See footnote 79 above.

82. "Jews," not Israelis or Zionists, despite the contention of the movement, and of other Arabs and Muslims for that matter, that they entertain no hard feelings towards the Jews as such and that their grievances are directed against the Zionists and the Israelis.

83. Jews are accused in Islam as forgerers of their Holy Scriptures; thus, they can easily falsify any other written material.

84. During the Lebanese War, Christian Phalanges entered those two refugee camps near Beirut and slaughtered many Palestinian civilians. Since then, the Arabs accused Israel of the responsibility for those massacres.

85. In August 1969, a lunatic Australian tourist, Michael Rohan, attempted to burn the Aqsa Mosque. Despite his indictment and trial, and the efforts made by Israeli authorities to extinguish the fire, Israel was accused by the entire Islamic world of that arson. Since then, that date has been commemorated annually, and the accusations are repeated each time about Israel's scheming in that tragedy.

86. *Dajjal* is not simply an imposter but the Anti-Christ in Islamic eschatological nomenclature. The Jews are implicitly accused of filling this role.

87. Khaybar is an oasis in northern Najd, where a Jewish settlement had existed for many centuries before the Prophet mounted an expedition against them in A.D. 628/9 and occupied their bastions. After that, the Prophet came into an agreement with them whereby they were al-

167

lowed to stay on part of their lands as serfs in return for half their annual crops. According to Arabic sources, the second Caliph, Umar (634-644), expelled the Jews from Khaybar altogether. Since then, Khaybar has become a symbol of Jewish submission to Islamic rule as long as they accepted it or to their expulsion if they do not. Many of the Hamas announcements during the intifada have indeed ended with the slogan: *"Hanat Khaybar,"* "The time of Khaybar has come!"

88. A three-stage program is hereby offered: first, to achieve freedom to say and do what they wish; second, to regain the territories under Israeli rule; and third, to "retrieve the rights," a code word for recuperating all of Palestine.

PART III: REVIVALIST ISLAM IN EUROPE AND THE FAR EAST

Chapter 8

MUSLIM MINORITIES UNDER NON-ISLAMIC RULE*

A contemporary authority in Islamic studies, Fazlur Rahman, worded the inexorable linkage between Islam and politics in one succinct sentence: "Islam, like communism, insists on assumption of political power, as the will of God has to be worked on earth by a political system."[1] No wonder, then, that Muslims are required (and as a rule strive) to live in a Muslim state. The minorities that fail to do so face very serious problems of identity, which at times end in crisis and unrest.

Muslims everywhere are aware that they belong to the universal ecclesia of Islam, the *umma*. At the same time, they lead a way of life that is bound to alienate them from their environment and engender suspicion from (and at times confrontation with) the host culture. Suspicion creates fear, and confrontation generates hostility, all the more so when Muslim minorities constitute either a local majority or a very substantial portion of the population in their host countries, thus exacerbating cultural hostility by adding economic competition and the threat of rebellion and secession.

From the viewpoint of the host society, if it can neither assimilate the minority nor drive it out, theoretically it must subjugate the minority or exterminate it. Muslim minority responses hinge not only on the inherent incompatibility between Islamic and non-Islamic rule, but also on the treatment meted out by the majority culture. When the Muslim minority is weak but the socio-political environment is liberal (like the United States), then pluralism is usually advocated by the Muslims, who thereby hope to win an existence on an equal footing with the majority. Under more oppressive regimes (like the Soviet or Chinese), the Muslim minorities are more likely to adopt the "assimilationist" course, that is, material acculturation into the host culture, while the core of the faith and community cohesion are kept intact. Indeed, the Muslim calendar, Muslim festivals, dietary laws and customs of worship inhibit anything more than a superficial assimilation.

The other possible responses of the Muslim minority are secessionism and militancy, and the two are often interrelated. When
minority Muslims are frustrated by the unworkability of a pluralistic
society (the former USSR's "Republics," Cyprus, the Philippines),
Muslims often become antagonistic, especially when the majority
transgresses the limits of uneasy coexistence and moves toward
outright subjugation or physical elimination. In such cases, the quest
for secession from the "abode of war" and reunion with the universal
"pax Islamica" can generate rebellion, which (if successful) strives
to attain political and cultural independence (Cyprus and the Philippines). Militancy entails more extremism than secessionism. A
militant Muslim minority not only seeks political and cultural autonomy, but also strives to dominate others, confident of its own
superiority (as in the case of Idi Amin's regime in Uganda). The
classic instance of militancy and secession is found in Muslim
history in Hindu India. Conquering Islam had subjugated Hinduism
and ruled the subcontinent. But when Muslim power was eroded by
the British, Islam sought and achieved separation from the Hindus
rather than submitting to the democratic rule of modern India that
would have allowed the Hindus to exercise political domination over
the Muslims. When the majority of Indian Muslims established their
own state (Pakistan), the *ulama* spoke of the reinstitution of the
Shari'a as the state law. There was no alternative to this arrange-
ment, if one bears in mind the fact that Islam is inconsistent with
other political ideologies. Maulana Maudoodi, the prominent Indian
Muslim modernist, has put it this way:

> To be a Muslim and adopt a non-Islamic viewpoint is only
> meaningless. "Muslim Nationalist" and "Muslim Communist"
> are as contradictory terms as "Communist Fascist" and "chaste
> prostitute."[2]

Thus, as orthodox Muslims see it, Islam is ideally an either-or
affair. Either Islamic law and institutions are given full expression
and dominate state life or, failing that, if the state is non-Islamic,
Muslims should try to reverse the situation or leave. In practice,
however, things are not so clear-cut. As long as an appearance of
peace and accommodation can be maintained, the minority Muslim
community, although entertaining a vague hope for the fulfillment of
its political aspirations at some future time, can contain the discrep-

ancy between reality and dream, and the tension between the two can go unresolved. But if persecution is intensified to the point where no real Muslim life can be ensured and if the practical opportunity arises, the minority Muslims are likely to seize it and proclaim either a separate Muslim entity or a Muslim state regardless of whether the Muslim population is a majority or a minority in the territory in question. For an Islamic state can encompass either. Muslims have experienced both a Muslim majority under non-Muslim rule, as in Christian Valencia where Muslims outnumbered the Christians four to one,[3] and a Muslim minority-rule in Hindu-majority India. It is Muslim rule, then, that defines the borders of the Abode of Islam, not Muslim minorities or majorities.

Let us illustrate these generalizations in China, Israel and Cyprus, particularly in the light of the current fundamentalist wave of Islam. These host countries illustrate the plight of minority Muslims under atheistic, Jewish and Christian rule, respectively.

The Muslim (Hui) Minority in China

The Muslim settlement in China dates back to the eighth century, and it underwent many vicissitudes in pre-modern times. Suffice it to say that by the eighteenth century, at the height of the Ch'ing rule in China (1644-1911), the Muslim community was strong enough to assert itself as one of China's recognized minority groups. However, unlike other minority groups, like the Mongols, the Tibetans and Chuang, the Muslims in China are not attached to any particular territory, although they admittedly constitute a majority, or a very sizable minority, in areas of the northwest. They can be found everywhere in China, and every large city is likely to have its Hui section. Thus, the Muslim problem in China stems not only from the aggregate figure of 30-35 million[4] all over China, but from their geo-demographic distribution, which makes any solution within an "autonomous region" an exercise in futility.

Furthermore, unlike other minority groups, whose home base may be included in toto within the confines of China (e.g., Tibet, Manchuria), the Muslims, whose focus of identity remains with the universal *umma* of Islam, regard themselves as a Chinese branch of an alien culture, not exactly a minority-guest culture in China. The daily validation of their membership in the *umma* is at the basis of

Muslim ritual, and one of the "Pillars of Islam" is the tenet of *haj* — the pilgrimage to Mecca, the holy place of all Muslims, the birthplace of the Prophet and of Islam. Nineteenth century China, which was marked by dynastic domestic decadence and by foreign incursions on its borders, witnessed a Muslim revival of unprecedented proportions, under the influence of fundamentalist movements that shook the Muslim world at that time. The ruling Manchu Dynasty condoned and at times even sanctioned the persecution of Muslims and other minorities, so much so that there was no escaping the collision course on which both sides were embarked. Indeed, during the nineteenth century, Muslim rebellions in China were rife, especially in the areas where Muslims constituted a majority of the population, and they threw many provinces into chaos. Unlike other rebellions, however, the Muslims did not want to take over the central rule in Peking or dismantle the dynasty; they were content to secede from the empire. One such heroic attempt was made by Tu wen-hsiu, a Yunnanese Muslim who shrugged off the Chinese order and declared an independent Muslim state in his province (1856-1873). Although this adventure turned out to be an ephemeral episode, Tu's use of Muslim symbols like "Sultan Suleiman" and "Commander of the Faithful," and the Arabic language in some of his proclamations bear witness to the latent vitality of repressed minority Islam.

Under the Communist regime, China has clung to the idea of the state as a unitary body politic, a concept that has its roots in the traditional view of the universe — the T'ien-hsia — ruled by the Son of Heaven. Thus, unlike the Soviet Union, which has recognized (at least in theory) the acceptability of a federation of Soviet Republics, many of which are populated by "minority" peoples, China has never budged from the traditional view that power emanates from the center; the center, in turn, is influenced by feedback from the masses below. In this setting, there is no room for political pluralism, although the Communist regime has taken cognizance of the cultural variety in China and has made serious attempts to recognize "minority nationalities" and to set up "autonomous regions."

From the 1950s onward, the radical line pursued in China with a view to communizing the economy and Mao-izing the sociopolitical behavior of the masses generated a head-on collision with the Muslim minority. *Waqf* (religious endowment) property belonging to the mosques was forbidden, and the educational system emphasized Marxism-Leninism-Maoism at the expense of Muslim customs and traditions. This policy generated strong opposition on the part of the Muslims who remained, on the whole, dedicated to their Islamic values and to universal Islam. A Muslim *imam* who escaped from China reported a *khutba* (religious sermon) that he had delivered to his congregation during those tough days:

> First, I outlined the historical facts of the struggles during the lifetime of the Prophet Muhammad and his final victory over tyrannical rule and evil powers. I entreated them to follow and to manifest the unconquerable and unflinching spirit of resistance of our ancestors.[5]

Moreover, in areas thickly populated by Muslims, where their self-confidence was compounded by overwhelming indignation, opposition to the Communist regime assumed a more violent character, to the point of open revolt.[6]

During the brief period of the "Hundred Flowers" (1956-1957), when open criticism was allowed, Muslims attacked the authority of the Communist party and the flood of Chinese migration into their areas, and some of them even demanded self-determination for their people in no uncertain terms. An official source acknowledged in 1958 that:

> The meeting of the Kansu Nationalities Affairs Committee took the view that local nationalism among the Hui was not only widespread but also pronounced in Kansu....Muslims denounced their fellow-Muslim Communist sympathizers as traitors to Hui nationality.[7]

Some Muslims discredited the fatherland concept cultivated by the regime, declaring that:

> China is not the fatherland of the Hui nationality....Arabic is the language of the Hui people....All the Hui people of the world belong to one family.[8]

Another official report revealed that:

175

The Hui declare that there is no living to be made in China, and even openly demanded emigration permits from the government so that they may return to Arabia to settle down. Some of them make it known that a government of *imams* will be established within an Islamic state.[9]

In May 1958, the *People's Daily* revealed that the Hui of Honan had twice revolted in 1953 and planned to establish an independent Islamic state. In April and June 1958, another Muslim movement, led by Ma Chen-wu, a Hui *imam* from Ningxia, erupted into a revolt with the reported purpose of establishing a "Chinese Muslim Republic" under the war slogan: "glory to Islam."

In the light (or obscurity, as may be one's worldview) of the Iranian revolution, these terms sound a rather familiar ring. But in the Chinese context, when one looks back to the history of Chinese Islam, one is struck by the repetition of the same traditional themes under Imperial and Communist China. To wit, Arabia — the place of inception and operation of the Prophet and of the faith — has remained in the Chinese Muslim ethos their true homeland, though neither they nor their forefathers had probably ever been there before. Their yearning is not merely to migrate to a land of safety, but to return to Arabia, as the only way for their physical and spiritual redemption. Similarly, the Arabic language, of which they know a mere trifle, has remained their language. For that is the tongue of the Prophet and the manifestation of the word of Allah as it descended to humanity in the Qur'an.

Despite these built-in tensions, there were times when the Communist regime ostensibly evinced benevolence towards its Muslim minority. The vacillations of China's policy toward the minorities in general and the Muslims in particular have been occasioned by a number of dilemmas facing Beijing's policy-makers:

1) The inherent contradiction between Communist ideology, which had raised high hopes among the Muslims for far-reaching self-determination, and the practical requirements of national interests that dimmed these hopes;

2) The built-in tension between foreign policy gestures toward the Islamic world and the demands of tough controls at home;

3) The acute contradiction between a crash integration program for the Muslims, which may give rise to resentment and uprising, and

a policy of liberalization, which may encourage their secessionist propensities.

Past experience has shown that in modern China, whenever Islam was oppressed to the point of jeopardizing its existence or when it was given enough leeway to express itself freely, voices of separatism came to the fore, at times violently. In order to avert Muslim uprisings in China, it is apparently necessary to maintain a precarious balance between a strong policy that does not encroach too bluntly on the cultural-religious viability of the Muslim community and a liberal and generous policy that remains short of virtual autonomy.

The Muslim (Arab) Minority of Israel

If the existence of a Muslim minority in a non-Muslim land is unenviable in general, how much more so in Israel, where the Arab Muslim minority (about .8 million out of 5 million) is torn between loyalty to its homeland and commitment to its Arab people — Israel's enemy.

Although the Arab-Israeli conflict is not religious in origin, the Islamic residue and symbolism that have become part and parcel of Arab attitudes toward Israel are shared, to a large extent, by Israeli Arabs. This problem is even more acute for the Arab Muslims who populate the territories administered by Israel since 1967.

These basic themes that are shared, in varying forms and intensities, by many Muslims across the globe have a direct bearing on the life of Palestinian Muslims. Even more than other Muslims who may feel resentment and frustration at their inability to reverse the situation, the Muslims living under Israeli rule sense the humiliation of being dominated by an erstwhile *dhimmi* nation with a questionable reputation in Islamic tradition.

Until 1967, the Muslim Arab minority in Israel was small in numbers and virtually isolated from the rest of the Arab Muslim world. Moreover, the Palestinian identity that was to gain prominence in subsequent years was faint and almost unknown to Israeli Muslims in those days. The Muslim minority seemed resigned to its fate; either out of despair or out of pragmatic considerations, it gradually drifted toward a long-term acceptance of its status as a minority culture. The war of 1967 reversed all that, largely because of the direct contacts between Israeli Arabs and their brethren in the administered territories, and because of the mounting stature of Palestinian identity.

This new link was dramatically epitomized in the events of April 1976, which came to be known as "Land Day." What was to be a protest by the Arabs of the Galilee against what they regarded as "expropriation of their land" became political agitation, and the Arabs' desire to maintain control of their lands was overshadowed by the irredentist slogan, "We shall liberate you, O Galilee!" This outburst, which resulted in loss of life, was accompanied by concurrent large-scale demonstrations in the cities of the West Bank, in support of the "oppressed brethren" in Israel proper. These disturbances were hailed throughout the Muslim world as an "uprising of the Palestinian people" on both sides of Israel's pre-1967 borders against "Israeli occupation."

This does not mean, of course, that all or most Israeli Arabs now side with the Palestine Liberation Organization (PLO) and have irreversibly relinquished their comfortable existence as a minority under Israeli-Jewish rule. As a matter of fact, many Israeli Arabs voiced their support of Israel and even rushed to help the Israeli authorities during the fateful days of October 1973. However, under the impact of the war and the rise of Islam, increasing numbers of Israeli Arab youth are more inclined than before to throw in their lot with the Arab Muslim population of the territories under the unifying umbrella of a "Free Democratic Palestine." This euphemism signifies, of course, that although "Muslims, Christians and Jews could live in peace," Muslim Arab hegemony would be resumed while the Jews and Christians would be relegated to their previous status of *dhimmis*.

The current revival of Islam has further exacerbated an already difficult situation. Internationally, an alliance between the PLO's Yasser Arafat and Iran's Ayatollah Ruhollah Khomeini prompted a new turn of events further Islamizing the Arab-Israeli conflict, drawing Iranian Muslims as well as Arabs into daily and actual involvement in the conflict. Arafat's battlecry in Teheran, "Today Teheran, tomorrow Tel-Aviv," and his public embraces with Khomeini, illustrate this point. In Israel and in the administered territories, more mosques are being built than ever before; more and more hitherto alienated youth are finding their way back to Islam; and a group of Muslim sheikhs has been pressing for the founding of an

Islamic college in Israel. Similarly, in the West Bank and Gaza, Islam has become a refuge for the frustrated Arabs who refuse to continue to live under Israeli occupation. The Muslim leadership (the Supreme Islamic Council) in the territories has been cultivating the virtue of persistence (*sabr*) in the face of adverse conditions, and occasionally incites a spiritual *jihad* as a purgatory process. As early as January 1979, a leaflet was distributed in Nablus urging believers to "join the Great Islamic Revolution that has been taking place in other lands of Islam."

To sum up, the Arab Muslim population of Israel and the Arabs in the administered territories have gradually drawn closer together, under the impact of Islamic revival and the impelling conditions of rising Palestinian nationalism and mounting Arab and Islamic confidence as a result of the Yom Kippur War. To contain this politically minded population under Israeli-Jewish rule as a minority devoid of national rights seems impossible. Unless some sort of autonomy or self-rule can be devised and accepted by the Arab Muslims in the territories, no lasting settlement can be envisaged. No such solution would be acceptable to the PLO and the Arab rejectionists, in any case. Therefore a reconciliation between Israel and its Arab population, within the pre-1967 borders (800,000) and in the administered territories (another 1.7 million), depends largely on the ability and willingness of this population to disagree with the other Arab Muslims who show no desire to see the conflict recede. Such a prospect seems dim and remote.

The Muslim (Turkish) Minority of Cyprus

Somewhat like the Arabs of Israel, the Turkish Muslim minority in Cyprus owes its allegiance to a motherland (Turkey) that lies outside the confines of its own territory; but unlike Muslims in Israel (who would like to see the Jewish state revert to the Abode of Islam in its entirety), Cypriot Muslims would rather secede from their Christian compatriots, who themselves strive for a Hellenistic Cyprus (*toksim* versus *enosis*).

The basic division of allegiance between the two parts of the Cypriot population is deepened by historical, ethnic, religious and linguistic stumbling blocks that keep those two groups apart. The Greeks of the island identify with the Hellenistic past, while the

Turks are direct descendants of the Ottoman conquerors; the Greeks adhere to the Greek Orthodox Church, while the Muslims follow Sunni Islam; the Greeks speak a local Greek dialect, while the Turks speak Turkish; the Greeks read Greek books and maintain a Greek curriculum in their schools, while the Turks read and study Turkish books; Greeks and Turks live in separate quarters or even separate villages; Greeks view the Turks as intruders and barbarians, the Turks regard the Greeks as cowards and selfish. Each of them considers its own group as a superior and more civilized race and looks down on the other.

Thus, the current struggle between the two groups, which echoes the historical struggle between Islam and Christianity in the Mediterranean and is intensified by nationalistic sentiments, makes the very idea of Cypriotism or local nationalism impractical. Even the magic word of self-determination cannot resolve the problem. "Self-determination" for whom? The Greeks would interpret it as the democratic rule of the majority; the Turks would claim that the enactment of democracy in the Western sense would perpetuate their domination by the Greek majority.

When Cyprus became independent in 1960, the Turkish minority (about 20 percent out of 600,000) was to share power with the majority, and the leader of the Turkish population held the office of vice president. But the Turks soon realized that they were relegated to a secondary role by virtue of their minority status in the general population, which viewed advancement on the political ladder as a function of ascriptive, not achievement-oriented, yardsticks. In other words, despite the similitude of democracy (which it was), united Cyprus under Makarios was a political system of ethnic communities and quotas rather than an open meritocracy.

Forced to choose between reconciling themselves to what they viewed as a servile second place in a Christian-dominated system or revolting, the Muslim Turks revolted. In fact, they had little choice, since Cyprus had been turned into a virtual Greek island, particularly after the rival communities put an end to dyarchy in December 1963. Bloody incidents burst out in that month in Nicosia and spread across the island.

The Greek Cypriots isolated the Turkish Muslim centers of population and disrupted the life of the minority by disconnecting communities, thus forcing the movement of some Turks to the security of larger Turkish Cypriot centers. Greek-held media presented the incidents to the public and to the world as a Turkish revolt against the republic, calculated to provide a pretext for Turkey to invade the island.

After December 1963, Muslim Turks evacuated their quarters in 72 mixed villages, abandoned 24 Turkish villages, and partially cleared out of 8 other mixed settlements. Moreover, in every one of the 6 mixed district towns, a partial evacuation of Turkish quarters took place. By 1970, about 20,000 Muslim Turks were registered as refugees with Turkish Cypriot welfare authorities.[10] Turks generally abandoned mixed villages in which they were in a minority, but they also abandoned some villages where they were the majority, since Cypriot-Greek troops had moved into those villages and in effect disturbed the local ethnic balance to Muslim disadvantage. If one takes a broader view of the majority-minority relationship, Turks gave way in the villages in which they constituted a majority when their minority status (and therefore their chances of survival) was considered in a regional context.

According to the Greeks, the major portion of the Turkish exodus from their settlements was initiated and directed by the Turkish master plan to facilitate ultimate partition. On the other hand, Turks claim that they had not developed any contingency plan for population consolidation, nor did they initiate the population transfers; rather, because they were intimidated by Greeks, Muslim Turks moved to the closest Turkish refuge they could find.[11]

Be that as it may, it is evident that except for the Nicosia enclave, where a strong Muslim quarter survived, the movement of refugees de facto created a Turkish-dominated area in opposition to the Greek-controlled land mass.

The intercession of United Nations troops in Cyprus contributed little to the permanent settlement of the conflict because the Greek Cypriot government of Makarios continued to rule high-handedly by the mandate of the Greek majority. For a time (1964), the government was prepared to encourage the return of Turkish refugees to their villages, provided they accepted its authority, and they did not return to sensitive areas. But the Turks, either frightened by the Greek majority, or because of *taksim* considerations, actually elected to perpetuate the de facto partition. The Muslim Turks, in sum, could not submit to Christian Greek rule in a situation where they themselves remained the minority. Paradoxically, as long as Cyprus was a British colony, Muslims accepted foreign rule, since their subservience was shared by all inhabitants of the island. But as soon as independence was granted to the island, Muslims could not accept the fact that other Cypriots would wield the reins of power, while the Muslim descendants of the glorious Ottomans would be pushed to the margin and might even be forced to rejoin Christian Greece.

Turks in Cyprus have consistently declared their readiness to allow their Greek compatriots to join Greece, provided they themselves exercise the same prerogative of joining Turkey. This double-*enosis*, which was put aside in 1960 in favor of an independent Cyprus, was revived again after 1974, when the escalation of intercommunal clashes made the Turkish invasion of the island inevitable. Turkey's intervention on behalf of Cypriot Muslims came when a military coup by the Greek Cypriots ousted Makarios in July. The coup was hatched and directed by the military junta in Athens, and Turkey saw the seizure of northern Cyprus and the regrouping of the Turkish minority there under Turkish guns as a self-defense measure. After the war, the Turks demanded a federal government in Nicosia where the Turkish minority would have an equal voice, or Turkish-Cypriot administration for six cantons in which local Turks would be regrouped. The Geneva talks failed and Turkish forces renewed their advance until they occupied more than one-third of the island. This occupation resulted in the flight of 180,000 Greeks southward to the Greek region while 100,000 Turks were regrouped in the north in houses abandoned by the Greeks. The Cypriot Turks were reinforced by a few thousand mainland Turks, under the pretext of the need for qualified agricultural workers.

Today, northern Cyprus is de facto ruled by Turkey, relying on a strong expeditionary force and the continuing strengthening of Turkish settlements in the north. On the declaratory level, the Muslim Turks of Cyprus continue to advocate either a federated state or total independence in the northern part of the island, but until that can be achieved, their dream of reuniting with Turkey (in nationalistic terms), or rejoining the Abode of Islam (in Islamic terms), has become reality.

Just as the Greek Cypriots cannot cease being Christian and Greek, the Turks cannot relinquish their Turkish and Muslim identity. Encouraged by nationalist-Turkish sentiment, Muslims cannot simply accept a Christian rule identified with Greek nationalism. If they had constituted the majority in Cyprus, they could have imposed an Islamic state without many qualms, but as a minority they would rather secede than yield.

Conclusions

Islam must ultimately assume statehood, because it is a way of life that inseparably encompasses politics and religion. When a Muslim minority happens to live in a non-Muslim state, it remains in many ways outside that state and nurtures separatist ideals that may materialize when the opportunity presents itself.

More recently, because of the mounting power and wealth of some Islamic countries, Islam has become a success story, something to be proud of. Moreover, the establishment of Islamic conferences, which have been convening annually since 1969, has lent a new impetus to popular if not political pan-Islamic sentiments. One may conjecture that the current Islamic impulse that has affected the length and breadth of the Islamic world will enhance the self-image of Muslim minorities everywhere, as has already been true in Cyprus, Israel, the Philippines, Thailand, Burma and other places. Muslim minorities across the globe are becoming more and more self-conscious, and mosques are sprouting in non-Muslim sites like Washington, London, Geneva and Seoul on an unprecedented scale and with untold splendor. Muslim minorities will become more and more aware of the legendary wealth and oil power wielded by Islamic countries, some of which, like Libya, have been backing Muslim separatist movements in Thailand and the Philippines. They will take a new look at the most powerful Islamic state, Saudi Arabia, where the Holy Places of Islam are located and where local sherifs claim descent from the Prophet himself. The Holy Pilgrimage (*haj*) will probably gain a new impetus; a growing number of Muslim pilgrims will make the journey to Mecca. For the first time, in 1979, even Israeli Muslims were allowed by the Saudis to join their brethren in the exhilarating Islamic experience of the *haj*.

In recent years, the enhanced stature of Islam has led the Muslim center to take a keener and deeper interest in the minorities on its periphery. This renewed interest manifests itself in the information printed in the Arabic press about Muslims in other lands, and particularly in the resolutions of the Islamic conferences, which have been bringing under one roof delegates from some 40-odd

Muslim countries and organizations representing over one billion faithful. Thus Philippines President Ferdinand Marcos recognized the Islamic conferences as a partner for negotiating the autonomy of the Moros. Other resolutions of that conference favored the Muslim community of Cyprus over the Christian Greeks and vowed the "liberation of Jerusalem" and support for the Palestinian Muslim cause.

Today's pro-Arab ambience in the world also generates a universal reluctance to antagonize Muslims. This was all the more true after the Soviet invasion of Afghanistan as the two world blocs catered to Muslim nations in order to attract them to their cause. Thus countries with sizable Muslim minorities will probably make an effort to liberalize their minority policy, taking the risk that more leeway for Muslim minorities might generate demands for autonomy.

Notes

* A version of this chapter first appeared in *Current History* (April 1980): 159-164, 184-185. The author thanks his research assistant, Carol Bardenstein, for her help in collecting the materials used in this chapter.

1. Fazlur Rahman, *Islam* (Chicago: Chicago University Press, 1979), Introduction.

2. Abu al'ala Maudoodi, *Nationalism in India*, pp. 5-11.

3. Robert L. Burns, *The Crusader Kingdom of Valencia* (Cambridge: Harvard University Press, 1967), p. 303.

4. There is much dispute about the figure. Estimates vary between 15 million and 80 million depending on the identity and political inclination of the author. Thirty million may be a fair assessment.

5. Kao Hao-Jen, *The Imam's Story* (Hong Kong, 1960), p. 14.

6. Yang I-fan, *Islam in China* (Hong Kong), pp. 71-78.

7. Dispatch of the New China News Agency, 16 January 1958. Cited by S. Ghosh, *Embers in Cathay* (New York, 1961), pp. 81-82.

8. *Ibid.*

9. *Ibid.*

10. See R. Patrick, *Political Geography and the Cyprus Conflict*, pp. 49ff.

11. *Ibid.*, pp. 77-78.

Chapter 9

REVIVALIST ISLAM ON TRIAL*

By an extraordinary coincidence, the end of 1989, which saw the turmoil in Eastern Europe climaxing in a virtual explosion of democracy and liberalism, also brought to public consciousness one of the many manifestations of obscurantism and bigotry which still plague our world. At the end of 1989, two trials were held in which militant Muslims were prosecuted for encouraging hatred and violence. In Stockholm, Sweden, Sheikh Ahmed Rami, the founder and director of "Radio Islam," was accused by the Swedish State Attorney of racist incitement against the Jews; in Israel, Sheikh Ahmed Yasin, the founder and leader of the Hamas movement in the Israeli-administered territories, was charged with subversive and violent acts against the Jewish state.

While the democratizing and liberalizing countries of the Eastern Bloc, who used to entertain scorn and hostility towards Israel, are now hastening to mend their relations with the Jewish people and the State of Israel, the Muslim militant fundamentalists make no secret of their burgeoning hatred towards both. Of course, the fact that democratization in some East Bloc countries is accompanied by popular (not government initiated) antisemitism by organizations like Pamyat is quite another story. It is our purpose here to examine the negative nature of the Muslim militant movement towards Jews and Israel and to suggest the common anti-Jewish denominator in the attitudes of the two sheikhs on trial. It is, of course, no coincidence that these two prosecutions unfolded in democratic societies, Sweden and Israel, where the legal systems protect freedom of worship and militate against institutionalized hatred and bigotry.

The Rami Case

On 15 September 1989, the Rami trial opened in the Stockholm District Court. The jury was to decide whether Rami, the Director of Radio Islam in Sweden, misused or misinterpreted the Old Testament's Pentateuch in a way that expressed contempt for the Jewish people.

If found guilty, he would be convicted of slander and libel towards an ethnic group, a crime punishable under Swedish law.

From the very outset, the accusation of ethnic slurs against the Jews was countered by Rami's defense on two grounds:

a) Freedom of speech, which could not be limited even when as a consequence someone may interpret it as slander;

b) All that Rami did, he contended, was to cite from the Bible, a holy document to all concerned, passages depicting the character of the Jews. If in these passages Jews turn out to be sexually perverse, sadistic, greedy, blackmailing, exploiting and criminal; that they stand behind organized crime and violence in the world; that they are drug dealers, pornography pushers, the producers of the pop music which has destroyed the youth in the West; and that they add fuel to wars in order to profit from them — so be it.

That Rami should utter all those anti-Jewish recriminations is no surprise in the context of his culture. However, that he sought the defense of "freedom of speech" from another culture which does not permit ethnic hatred and slander seems quite contradictory. In any case, a whole gallery of experts were produced by both the prosecution and defense in order to substantiate or refute the two claims advanced by Rami and his attorneys. In the process, the wider issues of the Arab-Israeli conflict were invoked, and the entire trial, if it did not actually become political, unfolded in a political context. Let us follow it step-by-step.

When the trial began it was stressed by the Swedish press that it was the "first time since the witch hunts that a Swedish court of law will take a position on the interpretation of the Bible."[1] What was at stake, according to the press, was whether parts of the Pentateuch were "expressions of racism, agitation and contempt against an ethnic group."[2] The prosecutor, Per Hakan Bondestam, decided to call to the stand Rabbi Morton Narrowe from the local Jewish community, and the former Stockholm Bishop, Krister Stendahl. Ahmed Rami, on the other hand, summoned as witnesses Jan Hjarpe,[3] a reputed professor of Islam at Lund University, and Jan Bergman, a professor of religion at Upsalla University. Hjarpe and Bergman eloquently made the point that the trial was aimed at silencing a certain political view on the Palestinian issue, not at attacking the Jews per se. Rami's statements, they contended, were primarily calculated to attack Israel, its politics and its role in world politics. Therefore, from their point of view, the trial concerned the limits of freedom of speech in Sweden, which they thought were not loose enough.[4] By so reasoning, they in fact concentrated not on using their Islamic expertise to refute the essence of the prosecution, but on challenging the entire premise on which Sweden had just adopted (in 1988) the new law about agitation against ethnic groups, following a convention of 1985 to which Sweden was a signatory and which condemned all propaganda which maintained that a certain ethnic group, or a certain color of skin, were superior to others, or which entertained prejudice against or called for racial hatred or persecution of an ethnic group. The prosecutor, based on this newly-adopted law, countered that mere derogatory statements about the reputation of an ethnic group or ridiculing it, even short of direct agitation against it, were enough of a legal justification to prosecute.

Bergman promised that his deposition in court would also compare Rami's interpretations of the Bible as applied to modern Israel with interpretations voiced by "extremist Jewish groups" in Israel; his assertion being that no one had the monopoly on the interpretation of the Bible, exactly as the Muslims held no exclusive right to interpret their Holy Qur'an. It was left to the jury to determine whether Rami's interpretations truly constituted a threat against or contempt of other ethnic groups, as defined by the new Swedish law. Some jurists argued that the law in question did not apply to "factual criticism," and that punishable responsibility can only be established when "factual discussion" is overstepped. That was precisely the case, according to Prosecutor Bondestam, and therefore the texts of Rami's broadcasts could clearly be defined as "persecution of the Jews." Put together in a negative context, biblical quotations could become "agitation against an ethnic group" and even overstep the blurred boundary between antisemitism and anti-Zionism, contended Bondestam.[5]

For Ahmed Rami and his lawyer, Ingemar Folke, it was eminently important to draw the limits between the concepts of antisemitism and anti-Zionism in order to justify the defendant's statement that he "did not care about their religion if it does not hurt us. I just wanted to give a voice to the other side in the Palestinian issue." He maintained that "criticism" against the politics of states is not agitation against the citizens in that state.[6] Some editorials in the Swedish press addressed themselves precisely to this line of defense when they specified that although Rami's programs had indeed contained virulent attacks against Israel's policies, one could not disregard their statements against Judaism as a faith or against Jews as an ethnic group. Some press articles argued that Sweden was free and open to political criticism of any country and even of blasphemous accusations against any faith, as in the case of Rushdie's *Satanic Verses*, but insulting or scoffing at a certain group of people must be forbidden. For example, they cited Rami's allegation that Jews were "possessed by sexuality, arrogant, demanding privileges and liars" and that the Nazi genocide of six million Jews was an "enormous propaganda bluff."[7] These accusations seemed so blatantly valid for prosecution that one columnist wondered about the "long time it took the Attorney General to make his decision to prosecute," when it was obvious that "a group of Swedish citizens of a certain religion were accused of being sexually obsessed, perverse and liars."[8]

Other columnists were incensed at those who wished to discuss the accusations against the Jews "in their political context," so as to deflect the argument from Jews to Israel and from antisemitism, a socially unacceptable indulgence, to anti-Zionism, a politically fashionable proposition. One of those columnists wondered what "political context" could be made of Rami's accusation that the "Jews conspired against morality and politics in non-Jewish societies," or his quotations from the *Protocols of the Elders of Zion*, or when he denied Jewish annihilation by Nazism in gas chambers. Wachtmeister, who had remarked in one of his articles in *Expressen* (23 October 1989) that it was "virtually impossible to separate antisemitism from anti-Zionism," was harshly chastened by one columnist who maintained that if Rami were to be acquitted, the "coarsest kind of hatred against Jews with a strong smell of Nazism of the 1930s would again become acceptable."[9]

As the trial unfolded, Bondestam demanded a jail term for Rami in view of the fact that he "has continued his antisemitic propaganda while he was being prosecuted," for which Swedish law (section 16:8 of the Criminal Code) envisaged a maximum two-year term. Two months into the trial Rami's attorney claimed that the defendant never went beyond "political, religious and cultural criticism" of Israel in both his broadcasts and his book *What is Israel?*. To substantiate Rami's contention that the Bible was used [by Israel] for oppression of the Palestinians, his attorney produced quotations by "extremist religious groups who had great influence in Israel." Since these groups were set against the Palestinians, the line of defense went, Rami had the right of solidarity with the Palestinians when he dismissed those quotations and produced his own, especially as he was dismayed by the Swedish and American fundamentalist Christians' support for Israel. He also argued that when he used the term "Jewish mafia," he did not mean all Jews but only "a small part of them, the Zionists."[10]

The defendant's attorney, Folke, implied that since Rami, a Moroccan and a Muslim, felt he did not bear any responsibility for the European Jewish victims of the Third Reich (whose crimes he had denied), he found it natural to identify with the Palestinians (also Arabs and Muslims) who had been "expelled by Israel." In his plea to vindicate his client, Folke attacked Professor Jorgen Weibull, one of the prosecution witnesses, who had likened Rami's utterances to Nazi propaganda, by "accusing" him of being "friendly to the Jews."[11] As the trial drew to its end, expectation generated a flurry of public reactions which were widely published by the Swedish press: from direct quotations taken from the broadcasts of Rami's Radio Islam, through an interview given by Israeli Judge Hadassah Ben-Ito, who visited Stockholm during the trial, to detailed coverage by the press across the country.[12]

On 14 November 1989, Rami was sentenced to six months in prison for "agitation against an ethnic group," after the District Court's verdict that Rami's statements were "clearly degrading and deeply offensive to Jews." The jury had indicted Rami on 18 of the 64 counts, but the defendant said he would appeal to the Court of Appeal.[13] Prosecutor Bondestam was satisfied with the outcome of the trial, and disregarded Rami's allegations that "Swedish society in general and the Swedish court system in particular are under Zionist influence," that the Attorney General would have "suited the Pinochet regime," and that Professor Jorgen Weibull, a major witness for the prosecution, was "actually a Nazi."[14] Radio Islam was to stop its broadcasts when the sentence was enforced, but Rami vowed that he would ask for a new permit to broadcast in order to implement his desire to "destroy Israel."[15]

The Swedish press, as a whole, hailed the sentence on the grounds that the offensive statements of Radio Islam against the Jews had nothing to do with the Arab-Israeli conflict, and that those statements indeed contained themes borrowed from Nazi (such as *Mein Kampf* and *Der Sturmer*) and other antisemitic publications, such as the *Protocols*, which "science has unanimously proved as forgery."[16] The Stockholm Community Radio Council allowed Radio Islam to pursue its broadcasts until 28 November, at which date it would decide the fate of the station, and it rejected the Radio's plea to extend its broadcast to 30 hours a week (6 hours a day, five days a week), as compared with the five and a half hours of broadcast allowed until then.[17] One columnist suggested that Radio Islam should be allowed to continue to operate in order to read aloud the names of the victims of the Holocaust. At a normal reading pace, the station would need three years in order to complete the reading of the lists, at a rate of forty hours a week, ten months a year.[18] The column also sarcastically suggested that if Rami were exhausted by the reading he could be assisted by his defenders, Professors Hjarpe and Bergman, who had contended that Radio Islam's antisemitic statements were "legitimate comments in the Middle Eastern debate."[19]

Ironically, Rami's propaganda backfired against him and his operators. Not only did he lose and saw his radio station shut down, but he unwittingly rekindled public interest in the Holocaust and in Israel. Not only were the Swedes reminded of Nazi horrors, once again, but pleas were invoked to understand Israel's role in the defense of today's Jews.[20] The Swedes also grasped the irony of Rami, a Muslim Arab, who viewed himself as an innocent victim of "witchhunting" and as a fighter for freedom of speech against other Swedes, "those hypnotized frogs and brainwashed parrots" who did not understand that he was their guarantee of freedom. Swedes began asking how they could have permitted the hate programs against Jews to go on, uninhibited, for three years prior to the trial.[21] But pending Rami's and Prosecutor Bondestam's appeals (the latter sought a longer jail term for Rami) and Radio Islam's closure, two Swedish organizations have applied for new Islamic community radio programs.[22] As these pages go to press, the legal battle has not yet concluded, but the proceedings in themselves show to what lengths Muslims are ready to go to fight against Israel and the Jews in order to discredit them.

The Yasin Case

Unlike Rami, who operated as an alien and member of a minority faith, Sheikh Yasin of Gaza, a native Palestinian, heads a local Muslim fundamentalist group which purports to struggle both for hegemony within Muslim-Palestinian society and for ridding itself of Israelis whom he and his followers perceive as usurpers of their land. Hence the totalistic and political nature of his message, even though much of his platform and many of his utterances bear a striking resemblance to Rami's writings and broadcasts.

Sheikh Ahmed Isma'il Yasin is paralyzed by illness, but his authority on Islamic matters is widespread. He is the acknowledged head of the Hamas, the Islamic Resistance Movement, a wing of the Egyptian-based Muslim Brothers, which took on the name "Hamas" at the outbreak of the intifada at the end of 1987. In 1984, Yasin had been sentenced to a long prison term when 60 rifles were seized in a secret cache in his house. He was released in 1985 as part of a prisoner exchange with the Gibril PLO faction, but he was barred from nominally reassuming his previous position as leader of the local "Islamic Association," the precursor of the Hamas. Until the intifada, Yasin was committed to religious and cultural activity among the Palestinians, but shunned any acts of violence or terrorist activity against Israel out of a clear realization that he stood to be quelled by the Israeli security machinery if he overstepped the boundaries of legality.

Apart from occasional interviews to the media, where Yasin discarded any possibility of a peaceful settlement with Israel, the thrust of the sheikh's thinking is believed to be expressed the Charter of the Hamas, published in 1988 in the territories, and which appears in translation in Chapter 7. In addition, several communiques have been published by the movement since the outbreak of the intifada, commenting on current affairs and laying down guidelines for the struggle against Israel. In both sets of documents the Hamas makes no secret of its goal to annihilate Israel through violent means and *jihad*, to be replaced by a "whole and indivisible Palestine" as a Muslim state.

That stance is not surprising and it is shared by many Palestinians on national and political, not necessarily religious, grounds. What is peculiar to Yasin's Hamas are the antisemitic broadsides which resemble Rami's (and other Muslim fundamentalists') attacks against Jews.

Based on this platform, which Yasin had purportedly helped formulate, as well as mounting evidence of actual Hamas participation in acts of terror against Israel, Yasin was arrested on 18 May 1989. The military court prosecutor accused him of membership in an illegal organization, of distributing hostile materials likely to incite the local population, and of calling for *jihad* against the Jews in order to retrieve Palestine. Yasin was charged with founding, heading, guiding, financing and directing the Hamas, which has embraced those objectives, and of taking an active part in recruiting, stockpiling weapons, and issuing operational orders to his disciples throughout the territories. In addition to 11 counts against Yasin, other members in the Hamas were also apprehended and prosecuted. By the end of 1991, the trial, which had been discontinued for political and security reasons, had not been resumed, and Yasin and his seized followers remained under arrest.

Conclusions

Despite the vastly different circumstances which surround the two trials in question, they have several common features:

1) Fundamentalist Islam almost invariably harbors a very deep resentment and hostility against Jews, Zionism and Israel. The difference between "normative" or "conservative" Islam and its "fundamentalist" brand seems to be a matter of degree and intensity rather than of values and basic tenets. The latter makes use of existing quotations from Islamic sources, demands their application here and now, and resorts to fiery and blunt language, while the former more pragmatically conceals, uses double language, and sometimes more conciliatory terms to deliver the same message.

2) Fundamentalists are intent on lumping together Jews, Zionists and Israelis. Further, the evil attributes of the one necessarily affect the others: the Jews being what they are — greedy, contriving, secretive, conspirators, corrupt and driven by a lust for their own power and a desire for the destruction of others — their movement of national liberation, Zionism, but above all their state, Israel, automatically derive their satanic features from the nature of the people who constitute them.

3) Fundamentalists are so persuaded of the absolute truth that they hold, that they cease regarding the world in relative terms, in terms of a multi-polar globe, pluralistic societies, coexistence of various faiths and political systems. Their world is one of Islamic dominion, of stereotypes of others, of condescension towards others.

4) Fundamentalists totally reject Western society and all its trappings; instead, they seek to establish a theocratic state based on religious law. They lean heavily on their holy scripture as the source of all knowledge and wisdom, and at the same time negate the claims of other faiths to their own scripture as a similarly valid source.

Rami and Yasin are only the tips of the iceberg that is fundamentalist Islam. Their cases became *cause celebre* due to their open trials which brought them to the attention of Western public opinion. One must realize, however, that much of the same vocabulary, stereotypes, objects of hatred, totalism, and uncompromising view of the world are shared by other Muslim fundamentalists in Iran, among the Muslim Brothers in Egypt, Syria and Jordan, by the fundamentalists of Algeria, Morocco and Tunisia, and by other revivalists of Islam in other places. Their anti-Jewish and anti-Israeli focus is only one facet of their multifarious rejection of the present world order. When allowed to do so, these movements can easily translate their antisemitic and anti-Israeli hatred into actual persecution and acts of violence and terror against Jews and Israelis.

Notes

* A version of this chapter first appeared in *International Problems* XXX:56 (1-2) (1991): 26-36.

1. *Svenska Kyrians Tidning*, 15 September 1989.

2 *Ibid.*

3. For the importance of Islamic imagery in Arab politics and in the denigration of Israel and the Jews, see that author's article "Religion and Political Legitimation in the Middle East," *Te Me Nos*, Studies in Comparative Religion, Vol. 18 (1982): 39-53.

4. *Svenska Tyrians Tidning, op. cit.*

5. *Ibid.*

6. *Ibid.*

7. *Vasterbottens — Kurieren*, Umea, 18 October 1989; and *Expressen*, Stockholm, 26 October 1989.

8. *Ibid.*

9. *Expressen*, Stockholm, 26 October 1989.

10. *Dagens Nyheter*, Stockholm, 2 November 1989.

11. *Dagen*, Stockholm, 2 November 1989

12. Examples:
A) *Kvallsposten*, Malmo, 5 November 1989, published excerpts of Rami's broadcasts:
1) Judaism is a criminal faith, accepted by a small and very unimportant tribe which has given birth to sadists and perpetrators of outrages. Jews are sexually perverse, sadistic, greedy, blackmailers, extortioners and criminals.
2) Jews are behind organized violence in the world. The Jews are the kings of narcotics and they have introduced pop music, the music that has destroyed the youth of the world.
3) The Bible of the Jews, the Old Testament, is a criminal so-called religion which inspires Israelis to oppress Palestinians.
4) Swedish cultural personalities are stooges of the Jews and of Zionism.
B) *Judisk Kronika*, Stockholm, 5 November 1989, quoted Ben-Ito as saying that "disaster would ensue if Rami were to be acquitted," because that would mean that hateful antisemitic propaganda was given legitimacy by a Swedish court.
C) See, for example, *Folket*, Nykoping, 6 November 1989; *Smalands Falkblad*, Jonkoping, 6 November 1989; *Vermlands Folkblad*, Kalstad, 6 November 1989; and *Lanstidningen*, Ortersund, 6 November 1989.

13. *Dagen*, 15 November 1989.

14. *Svenska Dagbladet*, Stockholm, 15 November 1989.

15. *Ibid.*

16. *Dagens Nyheter*, Stockholm, 15 November 1989.

17. *Dagens Nyheter*, 16 November 1989; *Dagen*, 17 November 1989.

18. The commemoration of the Holocaust worldwide, on 22 April 1990, curiously heeded that advice and held public readings of lists of the victims.

19. *Svenska Dagbladet*, 25 November 1989.

20. *Vestmonlands Lans Tidning*, Vasteras, 2 November 1989. See also *Ostgota Correspondenten*, Linkoping, 16 November 1989; *Svenska Dagbladet*, Stockholm, 19 November 1989 and 24 November 1989; and *Kyrkans Tidning*, 6-12 November 1989.

21. *Dagens Nyheter*, 4 December 1989.

22. *Dagen*, 6 December 1989.

Postscript

THE TURMOIL THAT LIES AHEAD

The Muslim fundamentalists' worldview does not limit itself to academic debates. It also requires action, through persuasion if possible, using violent means if necessary. This may have staggering consequences for Israel, the Middle East and the world. Firstly, a religiously-motivated Muslim is likely to act far more boldly and with far more sense of self-sacrifice than a politically-oriented guerilla/terrorist. The *fida'i* tradition in Islam can make death a desirable end unto itself, a happy way to reach the hereafter, as has been evidenced by events in Egypt, Lebanon, the territories, and even inside Israel. Such fundamentalist groups can be or become committed to the redemption of Islam through violence. Since they cannot operate armies in an all-out *jihad*, they can use individual terrorism, as some already do, both against domestic regimes in Islamic countries and foreign interests such as those of the U.S., Europe and Israel.

Israel and the West have to be prepared for the notion that liberalization in the regimes of Muslim countries, if and when it occurs, does not necessarily mean a democratic revolution of the type we have been witnessing in Eastern Europe. When one liberalizes one's regime, one is expected to give vent and to respond to popular sentiment. It turns out that in all cases of liberalization in Algeria, Egypt, Jordan, and the administered territories, to name only the most prominent examples, public sentiment proves its leanings toward Islam much more than toward national or personal allegiances. It also turns out that the thin veneer of modernity, Westernization and nationalism that some of those autocratic regimes, monarchical or military, had applied on their societies has been much more fragile than anyone could anticipate. In the case of Israel, itself not one of those tyrannical regimes, the Muslim revival is linked with the political and cultural resentment that Israeli Muslims entertain against the Zionist and Jewish nature of the state. In other countries, the rulers are caught in their fear to pursue the course of liberalization lest they be swept from power by the fundamentalists (see the cases of the Shah and Sadat), and therefore they try to mobilize the Muslim establishment to their side and they often succeed (Nasser, Sadat, Mubarak and others). This in itself alienates the masses from both the rulers and the submissive hierarchy of traditional *'ulama*, and gives further impetus to the rise of popular-fundamentalist Islam which clusters around adored *imams* outside the hierarchy.

Muslim fundamentalists do not and cannot advocate an innovative revolution to set up a democratic-like society, but a restorative revolution that harks back to the supposedly ideal order that existed in the times of the Prophet Muhammad and his immediate successors. Therefore, democratization in the Western sense is not to be expected to counter or alleviate the threat of Muslim fundamentalist pressures in such countries. The fundamentalists can easily sway the masses to their side because they can show that their societies are corrupt and degenerate, ruled by power-hungry and ruthless autocrats. But they also reject the West totally, including the idea of democracy, since the concepts of sovereignty and law-making that are inherent in the people's rights in the West reside solely with Allah, according to pious Muslims. They want to substitute for the tyrants who oppress them the rule of divine justice that only Islam can provide. This is what they mean when they profess their slogans of "Islam is the alternative," "Islam is the solution," and "Islam is the truth."

This is the reason why the leaders of Islamic countries face a terrible problem of legitimacy. They know that they rule not because they were chosen by anybody or that they inherited the mantle of the caliph, but despite the fact that they cannot lay claim to either. They rule by sheer force and therefore they must either continue to act ruthlessly and survive, or succumb to fundamentalist pressure from below, as the events in Iran demonstrated more than a decade ago. The Muslim Brothers in Egypt, who were not allowed to run for elections as a party and in 1990 boycotted the elections altogether; those in Jordan who ran and were elected as individuals; those who ran and succeeded in the Algerian elections; or those who defy the PLO in the territories, under the heading of the Hamas, or Jewish rule in Israel itself; all are openly challenging the legitimacy of the rulers of those countries. Thus the West does not have much to look forward to. If the present autocratic regimes persist, they will continue their basically anti-Israeli stance and deep suspicion of the West, given their present-day reliance on Western financial and military support which temporarily blunts that hostility. They must pursue this course not only due to the risk of totally losing their legitimacy in the eyes of their people, but also because of the nature of the West which fosters democracy, civil rights and liberal standards of rule, which expose them as backward and out of tune with the times. Conversely, if the Muslim masses, instigated by the models of Eastern Europe or, more significantly, of Iran, were to rise against their rulers, then the Muslim fundamentalists are the best organized and the most popular power to present a credible alternative.

The Second Gulf War (1991) and the atomization of the Soviet Union have shown how those trends can acquire global dimensions. In the first instance, Saddam Hussein, conscious of the anti-Western sentiment inherent among Muslims, made an appeal to *"jihad"* to the Muslims of the world, spelling out his commitment to fight for all Muslims against the "new Crusaders" who have not only lent support to Israel in Palestine but have dared to "invade" the Holiest of Holies of Islam, namely the land of Saudi Arabia, the core of Islam, the birthplace of the Prophet and the location of the holy cities of Mecca and Medina. These appeals were heeded by masses of demonstrators in the streets of Amman, Algiers and Islamabad. Baghdad's defeat was taken by many as Islam's defeat, hence the growing resentment and the calls for revenge voiced in many Muslim fundamentalist quarters.

The dismemberment of the Soviet Union has brought about the rise of "Islamic nationalism" in at least some of the six Muslim republics (Azarbaijan, Kazakhstan, Turkemenia, Uzbekistan, Tadjikistan, and Kirghizia). We already hear of Uzbek and Tadjik nationalists who have been trying to weave into a powerful fabric their ethnic sentiments with their revived Islam. This trend, which is reinforced by, and in turn feeds into, the current universal rise of fundamentalist Islam, where religion and politics are inexorably linked, is bound to take on an anti-Israeli bias, as has been the case with Iran, a non-Arab country, which stands today at the forefront of anti-Israeli rhetoric and action. If the trend of re-Islamization continues, as the relatively free elections in Jordan (1989) and Algeria (1991) indicate, there is little doubt that the years ahead will be quite risky for both the West and Israel.

SELECTED BIBLIOGRAPHY

Altman, I., "Islamic Movements in Egypt," *Jerusalem Quarterly*, No. 10 (Winter 1979).

Azmeh, Aziz, "Islam: The New Dawn," *Middle East* (November 1979).

Barreau, Jean-Claude, *De l'Islam et du Monde Moderne* (Paris: Le Pre aux Cleves, 1991).

Charnay, Jean-Paul, *L'Islam et la Guerre* (Paris: Fayard, 1986).

Dekmejian, Hrair, *Islam in Revolution* (Syracuse: Syracuse University Press, 1985).

Enayet, Hamid, *Modern Islamic Political Thought* (Austin: University of Texas Press, 1982).

Esposito, John, ed., *Islam in Asia* (New York and Oxford: Oxford University Press, 1987).

——, *Voices of Resurgent Islam* (New York and Oxford: Oxford University Press, 1985).

——, *Islam in Transition: Muslim Perspectives* (New York and Oxford: Oxford University Press, 1982).

Green, D.F., *Arab Theologians on Jews and Israel* (Geneva, 1974).

Haddad, Yvonne, *et al.*, eds. *The Islamic Impact* (Syracuse: Syracuse University Press, 1984).

Israeli, Raphael, T*he Public Diary of President Sadat*, 3 vols. (Leiden: Brill, 1978-79).

——, *Islamic Fundamentalism in Israel* (London: Brassey's, 1992).

——, *Peace is in the Eye of the Beholder (Images of Israel in the Arab Media)* (Berlin and New York: Mouton, 1985).

Jansen, G.H., "Militant Islam: The Historic Whirlwind," *New York Times Magazine* (6 January 1980).

Johnson, N., *Islam and the Politics of Meaning in Palestinian Nationalism* (London: Kegan Paul, 1982).

Keddie, Nikki, *An Islamic Response to Imperialism* (Berkeley and Los Angeles: University of California Press, 1983).

Kepel, Gilles, *La Revanche de Dieu* (Paris: Seuil, 1990).

Kramer, Martin, *Islam Assembled* (New York: Columbia University Press, 1986).

Lazarus-Yafeh, Hava, "Contemporary Fundamentalism in Judaism, Christianity, Islam," *Jerusalem Quarterly*, No. 47 (Summer 1988): 27-39.

Lesch, A. and Tessler, M., "The West Bank and Gaza: Political and Ideological Response to Occupation," *The Muslim World*, Vol. 77, No. 3-4 (July-October 1987).

Lewis, Bernard, "The Return of Islam," *Commentary* (February 1975).

——, The Political Language of Islam (Chicago: University of Chicago Press, 1988).

Mayer, Thomas, "The Military Force of Islam: The Society of the Muslim Brothers and the Palestine Question, 1945-8," in Kedouri and Haim, eds., *Zionism and Arabism in Palestine and Israel* (London: Frank Cass, 1982).

——, "Muslim Youth in Israel," *The New East*, Vol. XXXII (1989): 10-11 (Hebrew).

Momen, Moojain, *An Introduction to Shi'i Islam* (New Haven: Yale University Press, 1985).

Nettler, Ronald, *Past Trials and Present Tribulations* (New York: Pergamon Press, 1987).

Paz, Reuven, "The Islamic Movement in Israel, following the Mayoral Elections," *Data and Analysis*, Tel Aviv University (May 1989).

Pipes, Daniel, "The World is Political! The Islamic Revival of the Seventies," *Orbis*, 24 (1980).

Rahman, Fazlur, *Islam* (Chicago: Chicago University Press, 1979).

Ruthven, Melise, *Islam in the World* (Oxford: Oxford University Press, 1984).

Shahid, M., "The Muslim Brotherhood Movement in the West Bank and Gaza," *Third World Quarterly*, Vol. 10, No. 2 (1988).

Sivan, Emmanuel, *Radical Islam* (New Haven: Yale University Press, 1985).

——, "Orientalism, Islam and Cultural Revolution," *Jerusalem Quarterly*, No. 5 (Fall 1977).

Stoddard, Ph., et al., eds., *Change and the Muslim World* (Syracuse: Syracuse University Press, 1981).

Voll, John, *Islam: Continuity and Change* (Boulder: Westview, 1982).

ANALYTICAL INDEX

ABOUT THE AUTHOR

Raphael Israeli is the author and editor of some 60 articles and 10 books on Islam, Middle Eastern affairs, China and the Muslim minority in China.

His works include:

1. *Man of Defiance: A Political Biography of Anwar Sadat* (Weidenfeld & Nicolson and Barnes & Noble, 1985).
2. *Peace is in the Eye of the Beholder* (Images of Israel in the Arab Media) (Mouton, 1987).
3. *Palestinians Between Israel and Jordan: Squaring the Triangle* (Praeger, 1991).
4. *Islamic Fundamentalism in Israel* (Brassey's, forthcoming).
5. *Islam in China: A Critical Bibliography* (Greenwood, forthcoming).

Dr. Israeli is a graduate of the Hebrew University in Jerusalem and obtained his Ph.D. in Chinese and Islamic Studies at the University of California at Berkeley. He presently teaches Chinese, Islamic and Middle Eastern History at the Hebrew University and is a Research Fellow at the Truman Institute for the Advancement of Peace. In 1992 he became Chair of the Department of East Asian Studies at Hebrew University, and is a Fellow of the Jerusalem Center for Public Affairs.